Dispirited

How contemporary spirituality
is destroying our ability to think,
depoliticising society and making
us miserable

Dispirited

How contemporary spirituality
is destroying our ability to think,
depoliticising society and making
us miserable

David Webster

Winchester, UK
Washington, USA

First published by Zero Books, 2012
Zero Books is an imprint of John Hunt Publishing Ltd., Laurel House, Station Approach,
Alresford, Hants, SO24 9JH, UK
office1@jhpbooks.net
www.johnhuntpublishing.com

For distributor details and how to order please visit the 'Ordering' section on our website.

ISBN: 978 1 84694 702 5

A CIP catalogue record for this book is available from the British Library.

Design: Stuart Davies

Printed and bound by CPI Group (UK) Ltd, Croydon, CR0 4YY

We operate a distinctive and ethical publishing philosophy in all
areas of our business, from our global network of authors to
production and worldwide distribution.

CONTENTS

Acknowledgements

This book was conceived during beer-garden conversations with Dai Jones and Jonathan Elcock, convivial psychologists from the University of Gloucestershire. Other colleagues also engaged with my concerns in similar locations. Dr Roy Jackson tolerated, with typical fortitude, my ramblings on these topics, most notably during our Spanish excursions. Dr William Large read and commented, at generous length, on drafts of this work. I would like to express my thanks to all of these good people, and also hope they can be considered largely to blame for any failings contained herein.

Thanks also to Mark Fisher for the title, and to my family – Anna, Holly and Jack – for tolerating my disappearance to cafes to write/eat cake during the summer when this book was completed.

Introduction

'Spiritual, Not Religious...' The case of spirituality without religion

When someone tells me that they are not really religious, but that they are a very spiritual person, I want to punch their face. Hard. But I don't; partly because it is a poor way to recruit students, and also because it is probably wrong. And I am a coward who fears retaliatory pain. But it does annoy me hugely. It annoys me because confusion is distressing – and when people tell me this, I really don't know what they mean. I do know what they mean in a socio-cultural sense. They are indicating to me that they don't want me to mistake them for one of those 'crazy' religious people – the sort who believe that they are right and other people are wrong, the type who is tainted by religious extremism and fundamentalism. They want me to recognise them, though, not as a shallow egotist with a mere mechanistic world-view, but as someone with depth and sensitivity. In this latter desire, 'spirituality' seems to the label-du-jour.

But beyond its use as a socio-cultural identification, I am unsure what empirical content to ascribe to the 'spiritual, but not religious' statement. Does it mean that the utterer has beliefs, but doesn't practice them in any way? Perhaps not. Maybe they mean that they are some type of syncretist who follows a path of their own faith-conflations – but I can't be sure. Largely I am confused, as I understand religion as a spiritual activity, and crucially, see spirituality as fundamentally religious in nature. I would suggest that to be spiritual, you *have* to be religious. Before I can move on here to a critique of spirituality, it would appear a certain amount of clarification will be required.

What does this label mean?

Trying to thrash out a definition of what 'spiritual' might mean turns out to be a thankless and largely fruitless undertaking. Jeremy Carrette and Richard King note: 'There are perhaps few words in the modern English language as vague and woolly as the notion of 'spirituality''.[1]

By itself, this is not a problem, 'love' can be pretty hard to define, and that is not enough to have us rejecting that it can mean something, and maybe, on a good, day, something positive. It is perhaps worth trying to get some sense of it, as Carrette and King recommend, by its usage. Perhaps the two most pertinent and persistent deployments of the term are as an element within two recurrent phrases. The first, proudly sat in bookshops next to 'Paranormal Romance' and 'Painful Lives' is the category 'Mind, Body & Spirit'; elsewhere we are often assaulted by the term 'Contemporary Spirituality'. Both these uses give us an insight into the meaning that users of the term 'spiritual' wish to imbue it with.

In Biblical manner, let the last be first – and we can return later to the Mind, Body, Spirit-world at greater length. The term 'Contemporary Spirituality' is intriguing, as it is broader than one might imagine. Indeed, to stay in a new-age mindset, it is rather holistic, encompassing both newer, less formalised and collectivised forms of religious practice, and attempts to breathe new life into existing, more traditional religious traditions. You will find a wealth of volumes, should your reading stray into catalogues from both popular and academic theological publishers, on contemporary Christian spirituality.[2] While Christianity appears to lead the field in this area, other faiths also describe themselves in terms of their either being a form of, or via an engagement with Contemporary Spirituality. We can read this as religious attempts to understand what it means – in the world we currently inhabit – to believe in a world which exceeds the material – a world of things both visible and invisible[3]. This is, in some ways, what the task of Theology has always been. When I arrived in the academic department I currently work in, I found myself working predominantly (to my slight surprise) with Theologians and experts in Church history – and one of my initial concerns was to work out what the hell Theology actually was – and the phrase that struck me as having the most explanatory efficacy – that really seemed to capture what it was that they sought to achieve – was 'faith seeking understanding'. In this sense – Theology is the attempt at finding out what it means *if* we accept certain foundational propositions. If we take on board specific fixed points – what does that do to the world, and our relation to it?

While I am not a rampant advocate of Christian Theology, or similar traditions in other faiths, they do seem to have an edge here on the Mind, Body, Spirit (MBS) approach – in which there is often the danger that there are too few fixed points from which to work. If all is open, provisional and truth is too syncretically constructed, the substantive challenges that plague Theologians seem to evaporate. While advocates of MBS spirituality might see this as an advantage, I will argue that this pick 'n' mix, or buffet approach to your beliefs is exceptionally problematic.[4] If beliefs are problematic, challenge preconceptions, appear to clash and contradict, then rather than the grindingly difficult work of theological exegesis, or hermeneutic analysis and painful reflection – you can just swap out the offending belief. Were I a cynic, I would go as far as to suggest that the spiritual quest for the Mind, Body & Spirit movement largely constitutes an attempt to blend traditions to suit one's lifestyle aspirations, rather than following a faith which makes you uncomfortable –and which is hard to believe, challenges your desires and goals for your life and asks more of you that you ask of it. By end of this book I hope to have persuaded you that this harsh-sounding characterisation is not only true, but that its consequences are wider, and potentially harmful, than we might initially suspect.

Medicine and Spirituality – A definitional aside

When reading about contemporary notions of Spirituality, one thing of note was how many of the sources online for defining and discussing spirituality were drawn from those involved in conventional medicine, looking for ways to provide more holistic care by meeting the spiritual needs of their patients. The USA's National Cancer Institute actually had one of the clearer definitions:

spirituality:

Having to do with deep, often religious, feelings and beliefs, including a person's sense of peace, purpose, connection to others, and beliefs about the meaning of life. [5]

This is a rather intriguing quote – and it captures many of the more positive aspects of what is sometimes classed as spiritual. It did strike me, though, that its contents were just as amenable to a post-spiritual reading. If we excise the reference to religion – I feel that philosophy, as practice rather than mere academic discipline, perhaps when supplemented by insights from psychology, might fit equally well. It is about feelings and beliefs – and relates to our connections to others, is directly concerned with the meaning and purpose of life, and extent to which peace is, or is not, desirable or attainable. These goals of reflection and deep consideration can be achieved entirely without the need to invoke some concept of 'spirit', which not only adds nothing to the content here, but which might actually endanger the undertaking. The way in which discourses of spirituality endanger the task of making sense of our lives, and our connections to others, is explored throughout the rest of this volume.

At the Huge Naidex event, a Healthcare exhibition and trade fair at the NEC in Birmingham, a module of Continuing Professional Development (CPD) for Healthcare workers on Spirituality[6] offers a discussion of the nature of spirituality, and makes reference to a huge, and growing, body of literature in this area. In the blurb for the session, the author states:

> Spirituality gives each person intrinsic worth, and this is expressed through engagement in meaningful and purposeful activity.
>
> So, again, it can be seen that our spirituality enhances the occupations we choose to undertake and gives meaning to these activities as in, for example, our feelings as we hold a new-born baby, design a garden and watch the plants grow, and meet with a familiar religious community to worship God together. [7]

What is interesting here is the sense that if we experienced these events, be it baby-holding or garden-design without a spiritual aspect to our lives, the implicit claim would be that we would have less of an experience – that spirituality is a value-added component of life. It is also offered as of pragmatic benefit – referring to the well-known study by Mueller, et al in Mayo Clinic Proceedings[8]. What is intriguing is that the Mueller study (a very detailed review of other studies, with close attention to detail) sets aside the question of truth altogether. It looks and asks a Nietzschean question: what is the impact on health of holding particular points of view? The study, *Religious Involvement, Spirituality, and Medicine: Implications for Clinical Practice*, is not unaware of this, and notes that this may well be the result of a Placebo effect. [9] An interesting line creeps in towards the end that rather made me think:

> The spiritual history helps the physician discern the spiritual needs of patients. Furthermore, such inquiry is a form of spiritual care in that it allows patients to voice their spiritual and existential concerns. [10]

What is here is the phrase 'spiritual and existential' – and I wonder whether for the ill, these are not the same, and to echo my previous point – we could strip out the notion of the spiritual without any loss at all? You can take an auto-biographical narrative from someone which touches on their concerns, sense of self, or meaning et al without presupposing that this is a 'spiritual' undertaking. Now – of course a patient may choose to introduce what they see as a religious / spiritual aspect into this – and in this context, that is very much their prerogative – but to presume that that this existential task is *intrinsically* spiritual seems exceptionally presumptive, exclusive and troubling.

A Dark Trinity

My overall aspiration here is not merely, or at all really, to dispute the existence of a 'spiritual' component in the psycho-physical phenomena of human beings[11]. Neither is it to rehearse increasingly tired, and tiring, arguments about a supposed clash between atheists, secularists and theists. What I find both more compelling, and more urgent, is the extent to which discourses of spirituality, from new-age' Mind, Body and Spirit' (MSB) advocates, and to a minor extent from within established traditions who propagate an account of their own 'contemporary spirituality', are intellectually and culturally harmful. I would go further, and at the risk of sounding alarmist and bombastic, suggest that these discourses are a form of poison that taints not only critical and social realms, but also does violence to our potential to be authentic, happy(ish)[12] and fulfilled human beings.

The three main concerns of this book then are the impact of spirituality on critical intellectual thinking, on our sense of the social and political, and the impact on the human potential for happiness and fulfilment. Throughout much of the first two chapters, I argue that the way in which spirituality is conceived of, represented and manifested clouds our ability to think clearly and makes unhelpful interventions in our understanding of the nature of truth.

Secondly, the inward turn, to the self, to journey on the spiritual quest, often involves a rejection of the mass of detail in the world and a re-evaluation of material, worldly concerns as somehow squalid, shallow and beneath the spiritual aspirant. The sinister consequence, I suggest, of this is that spirituality can be an engine of depoliticisation. There is often a critique within contemporary spirituality of consumerism, seeking happiness in things, and of an unthinking life of sensual self-indulgence. I, like many others, see value in such a critique – but fear that spirituality is a dead-end of a response. It is a response that is a fleeing from these things – not an engagement with them. Spirituality cedes the world to the worldly. It misses the opportunity to renegotiate the nature of what it is to be worldly, and of the world. Fleeing down an avenue of detachment from the world, we are at danger of not only leaving political and social justice behind us, but along with the flight from reason alluded to earlier, there is a danger of descending into a self-regarding and relativistic sentimentality, driven by a solipsistic emotionality.

To complete this dark trinity, I will claim that immersion in, and affiliation with, the contemporary spiritual milieu is unlikely to make us either happier or more fulfilled. That it is a dead-end of bad-faith for human fulfilment. What I propose is that spirituality fulfils, although with more troubling consequences, the same precise existential function as train-spotting, stamp-collecting, triathlon competing, and home-improvement television. That is, it is an attempt to obscure from view that which lies directly ahead of us: our own death. In spirituality there are two aspects to this death-denying – metaphysical and psychological. The metaphysical is more plain, but also more disingenuous. It is the claim that we have an (eternal) spirit, which will survive the death of the body (and brain) and live on in a non-material realm. Beyond mere concerns with the philosophical coherency of such assertions, I have grave doubts as to the confidence of those who allege that they possess such views. Do people *really* believe that they will survive their own death? It may be a psychological failing on my part – but I find it almost impossible not to believe that such beliefs are not filled with dread and doubt. Confidence in post-mortem existence is deeply troubling, and I suspect it may not, except in perhaps a few deeply-conditioned religious practitioners, even exist.

On a psychological level, and this is where the connection to obsessive 'hobbies'[13] comes in, the preoccupation with the spiritual life, and living it as a 'lifestyle' fills the mind with details. It floods us with ideas, revisionist religious histories, techniques to learn, specialist vocabularies to acquire, and prevents us thereby seeing what we wish not to see. I am all too familiar with this, prey to 'enthusiast' magazines, and their innovative and welcoming deployments of specialist nomenclature[14]. The MBS type of spirituality seems wholly awash with this.[15] Everywhere there is terminology, product, and detail; be it at the very commercial *Spirit and Destiny* magazine end of the spectrum, or in the specialist healer's supply catalogue. Mind, Body and Spirit Fairs are found, like a rash, over the land. What they offer seems like a parody or mirroring of academic activity: lectures, seminars, books, journals and conferences. Along with this, the aspirant is offered an alternative account of history, a new lens through which the past can be seen.[16] That's a lot to take in – and will do the job as well as any doll-house furniture or hiking equipment catalogue.

Spirit as Metaphor

Of course, not every instance when 'Spirit' is invoked is necessarily an attempt to conjure up metaphysical essences. Often, probably more often than we realise, references to the 'spirit', to being 'spirited', or even to taking a 'spiritual' approach are metaphorical, using the term as a form of shorthand to refer to what I would suggest are often certain, ultimately psychological, phenomena. 'Spirit' can act as way of referring to a blend of character traits, or virtues. These might include determination and commitment ("he's got spirit, I'll give him that". Or "despite their defeat, Sunderland gave a very spirited performance in Tuesday's game"). It might refer to your most pervasive and defining facets ("that funeral service captured Dave's spirit, his sense of fun and joy"). 'Spirit' is often used to refer to something hard to describe, to capture and put into words ("that was in the spirit of the game, though it broke about three rules at once", or "Holly's contribution was very much in the spirit of the project, despite its impracticality and prohibitive cost"), or some original intent that we struggle to articulate ("while her intervention may have technically been outside the law, it was very much in its original spirit").

These examples demonstrate that we often deploy 'spirit' to refer to that which is hard to quite capture without a lengthy digression. It can refer to aspects of a phenomenon which is somewhat amorphous and pesky to articulate. Nonetheless, that does not mean that that which is referred to is *actually* ineffable. Much of the time, I am convinced that we handle spirit-as-shorthand quite happily – recognising it for what it is. However, there seem to be two exceptions. The first is when we refer to 'the Human spirit' – which is more ambiguous. Secondly, of course, is when we run up against the term as 'spirituality' – which seems to have grown into a more explicit denoting of some mind-body transcending phenomenon.

The Human Spirit is not a thing; it is, when it has been used at its best, a means for articulating a particular way of Being. When writers such as Pierre Hadot have talked of the spiritual life[17], they are not introducing, or asserting, crude metaphysical entities. What they seem to be doing is using the term to refer to a way of orientating yourself to reality/life. Hadot's account of the 'spiritual exercises'[18] he discusses in seems to be about being reflective, thoughtful and in some ways more rational, about what you *really* want, expect and believe you deserve in life. The point of these exercises is not to liberate our 'spirit', but something altogether more noble:

> Thus, all spiritual exercises are, fundamentally, a return to the self, in which the self is liberated from the state of alienation into which it has been plunged by worries, passions and desires. The "self" liberated in this way is no longer merely our egoistic, passionate individuality: it is our *moral* person, open to universality and objectivity, and participating in universal nature or thought. [19]

I could, you might suggest, call off my attack, lobbying instead for a broad redefinition of the term 'Spirituality' – a linguistic reclamation. While Hadot manages to use the term in an incredibly positive way, and does this with some panache, I fear we are, as a culture in general, less capable of such a nuanced use of the term. The notion of the spiritual as affiliated with the Mind, Body and Spirit movement, or at the least as implying the reality of an essence which precedes material existence, is too deep rooted in our culture. To deploy spirituality in the twenty-first century is to warp an ontological orientation into a crude metaphysical essence. By the end of this project, we might just locate better, less confusion engendering, terms for 'the human spirit' which captures its positive uses, with fewer of the risks I seek to here outline.

Introducing the idea of an existential post-spiritual world view.

So if we want to exclude spirituality from realist discourses, corralling it in the pen of metaphor – just what kind of world are we left in? The word that seems to race to mind in such a context is 'bleak'. That is – the world without any spiritual reality is often conceived of as an ethical scorched earth – an endless desert devoid of any teleological coherency or purpose. Oddly, perhaps, the image that I find particularly compelling in this context is a Biblical one – less odd though that it should be drawn from the book of Ecclesiastes (1.2-11)[20]:

2   Vanity of vanities, says the Preacher,
      vanity of vanities! All is vanity.

3   What does man gain by all the toil
      at which he toils under the sun?

4   A generation goes, and a generation comes,
      but the earth remains forever.

5   The sun rises, and the sun goes down,
      and hastens to the place where it rises.

6   The wind blows to the south
      and goes around to the north;
      around and around goes the wind,
      and on its circuits the wind returns.

7   All streams run to the sea,
      but the sea is not full;
      to the place where the streams flow,
      there they flow again.

8   All things are full of weariness;
      a man cannot utter it;
      the eye is not satisfied with seeing,
      nor the ear filled with hearing.

9   What has been is what will be,
      and what has been done is what will be done,
      and there is nothing new under the sun.

10   Is there a thing of which it is said,
      "See, this is new"?
      It has been already
      in the ages before us.

11 There is no remembrance of former things
nor will there be any remembrance
of later things yet to be
among those who come after.

Now *that* is bleak. Here is a world where all we do turns only to dust, and is forgotten – nothing we do seems to mean anything – it's just a passing, repetitious, churning world of generations rising up, only to be hacked down by indifferent mortality. But this is not in any sense a new problem; the author of Ecclesiastes foresaw it, Sartre expressed it when he asserted that we begin with the realisation that *existence precedes essence,* and Albert Camus put it best. Of course. At the outset of *The Myth of Sisyphus,* Camus asks us whether life in such a world is worth living:

> There is but one truly serious philosophical problem and that is suicide. Judging whether life is or is not worth living amounts to answering the fundamental question of philosophy. All the rest – whether or not the world has three dimensions, whether the mind has nine or twelve categories – comes afterwards. These are games; one must first answer.[21]

Why is this the primary question? Because of the world we occupy. The world just is what it seems to be to the author of Ecclesiastes. So what can we do? Camus finds a way through this – he sees the realisation of this world as a challenge. I see it as a choice as he does – between suicide and a remade sense of self where we choose to face up to the reality of nihilism – and work at living well anyway. Isn't this what Camus has Sisyphus do?[22] He finds a way to live well in his mind, while acting out a life he knows to have no intrinsic meaning.

I want to consider here the idea that facing up to the bleak, nihilistic, brain-numbing pointlessness of life is the best way to work towards a well-lived life. A student[23] last year compared Camus' Sisyphus' determination to be content, or happy, to the conscious adoption of a specific attitude to life within the Sikh tradition – the idea of *chardi kala* - a self-enforced positivity in the face of difficult times. This seemed distinct from the 'positive thinking' movement in that it didn't foresee that the attitude would solve any of the problems. Rather it was the voice of generations advising that these things *can* be borne. My goal here is not to merely indicate the dangers of spirituality, but to also begin to see what it means to be pioneers in the blasted landscape of the post-spiritual. Have we the strength for the task: to imagine Sisyphus and ourselves happy? Can we concur with Camus on the power of thought to overcome the absurdity of our own futility: '*But crushing truths perish from being acknowledged[24]*'?

Straw Men of Spirit?

Some may accuse me, in either parts or all of this book, of a Straw Man/Aunt Sally claiming that I set up only the most crude stereotype of spirituality to make it all the easier to knock down. The reader will have to judge, but while there *are* more subtle accounts of spirituality in use, many of these might be argued to reply on a largely metaphorical use. Further to this, if I am looking at the social impact of spirituality in its board form, then it is the popular expression of this that should rightly be my concern. My position is that the more subtle, humane and considered a form of spirituality is, the less it actually needs to rely on notions of 'spirit' at all, and the nearer it edges towards the kind of neo-existential, post-spiritual philosophical outlook that I advocate by the end of this book.

Chapter One

The Rise of Spirituality
Spirituality as an alternative to formal religious practice

As noted earlier, Jeremy Carrette and Richard King offer a useful, and critical history of 'spirituality' in *Selling Spirituality*[25], and one of the most important features that they note is the emergence of the term, despite its lurking presence since the seventeenth century, in late nineteenth and early twentieth century thought. This emergence relates to tensions between conventional, organised religious traditions, and a sense of a 'spiritual life' which seemed ill-served by such institutionalised traditions. Combined with an influx of ideas from further afield (some such as Swami Vivekanada actively promoting the idea of the spiritual, and opposing it to Christianity[26]), and on-going social change, the idea of 'spirituality' has seen mass growth, coinciding with a decline, in the UK, of the observance of traditional Christian forms of practice. Paul Heelas and Linda Woodhead, in 2005, published *The Spiritual Revolution: Why Religion is Giving Way to Spirituality*, based on fieldwork in Kendal. While their conclusions were less conclusive than the title suggests, they make a range of well-evidenced and interesting points. Early in their research they fix on the idea that the 'holistic milieu' (as they call it) is dominated by a desire for subjective ways of thinking – for self-discovery, and deeply personalised (and therefore unquestionable) accounts of truth:

Time and time again, we hear practitioners rejecting the idea that their relationships with group members or clients have anything to do with pre-packaged, or what we are calling in this volume 'life-as', ways of transmitting the sacred. Statements like that of homeopath Beth Tyers, 'I certainly don't have a fixed faith or dogma I adhere to' were typical. So were words to the effect of shiatsu practitioner Jenny Warne's affirmation, 'We don't want to be something we impose on somebody else'. [27]

This seems to capture something central about the contemporary forms of spirituality that I am interested in here. Spirituality is an account of a non-material component of the Universe, which is so ineffable as to be inexpressible, in such a way that debate, imposition, argument and disagreement become meaningless and fruitless. This strikes me not as a reasonable level of tolerance, or open-mindedness, but rather as a wilful flight from sense and reason into an intellectual space where believing you are correct, and others are wrong is somehow seen as a badge of spiritual immaturity.

Spirits, Spiritualism and Spirituality

Spirituality is, in itself, an interesting term. Allied terms have a sometimes confusing range of meaning. 'Spirit' is in widespread use as a metaphor for the more ineffable, subtle, and sometimes motivational aspects of the mind-body nexus – in its linguistic deployment as 'the human spirit' – or other metaphoric uses such as 'spirit of the age', 'team spirit', and many more. I, of course, have little problem with this, being concerned only when the notion of spirit becomes concretised as some form of metaphysical reality as an essence, or object. Some might argue that the term 'spirituality' is equally capable of metaphoric deployment, but I remain sceptical regarding this claim in terms of its actual use. Particularly given the rise of its use in Mind, Body and Spirit contexts and within more longstanding religious traditions, the use of the term 'spirituality' such that the existence of a spiritual entity is not either presumed or implied is very much the exception[28], rather than the norm.

It is important to consider another use of the term – which has some influence on the broader use of 'spirituality' which is 'Spiritualism'. Given the rather vague, flexible and confusing uses of spirituality – 'Spiritualism' is much more specific – referring to a very particular branch of Monotheistic supernaturally focussed religion. It is interesting in that it styles itself, despite its otherworldly focus, as empirically grounded. In the definition on the UK Spiritualists' National Union website they write: 'Spiritualism is a science because it is based upon proven facts that can be demonstrated and scientifically classified.' [29]

While the focus on souls, spirits and angels may seem rather post-1960s, especially given the explosion in Mind, Body and Spirit-style books, and more related to angels in the first decade of the 21st Century, Spiritualism is not only much older (tracing its roots as a formal organisation to the mid 19th Century[30]) but also more formal. Spiritualism has churches, set beliefs, membership and meetings. In many ways it has replicated the structure of many Christian denominations of its time. What is notable here, and the real reason I think that the Spiritualist Church is worth addressing, is that despite a whole industry of publishing, therapies and workshops that shares many of its core beliefs – mediumship, spirit communication, angels and a semi-mystic victim-mentality account of religious history, the Spiritualist Church has continued to see its membership decline. Those buying angel books, reading *Spirit and Destiny* magazine, attending seminars and workshops at their local holistic centre; these people have not felt at all drawn to the Spiritualist Church. If we want to know why this is – I would argue that it is largely a matter of form, of style, of social patterns of engagement with institutions rather than a matter of content. Given the disregard in MBS circles for concerns over conflicting spiritual truth-claims, it is unlikely to be as a result of a conceptual or doctrinal misalignment. The Spiritualist Church though demands the things that the new age / MBS movement is not comfortable with: membership, regular attendance, and *it looks like going to church* – and fails to fit with a sense of being 'alternative'.

Faith-Lite?

As I have tried to allude to already, the iteration of spirituality represented by the 'spiritual but not religious' approach can be accurately characterised as 'faith-lite'. This may seem harsh, or unfair, but I am convinced that there are good reasons for asserting this so boldly. The traditional religions, as we are all familiar with, have certain negative associations that make many uncomfortable in affiliating with them. But this is not the only reason for the growth of 'spiritual but not religious'. Another key social driver in this context has to be the sense in which we live in an ever-increasing age of personalisation.

This is not mere individualism, but is something more where people wish to see their life experience not as a generic, stamped-out, same-as-others narrative – but as something more bespoke, designer, branded and unique. That may sound over-put, but think of how we have come to consume media. I only take the TV cable package that suits my preferences, my Tivo box can detect and act on my preferences and personalise my experience. My twitter account allows me to only subscribe to those writers and news sources that I find palatable – and as my preferences change, I can silently unfollow and adapt the incoming information stream to suit me. [31] My on-line book retailer knows what I will enjoy, and if my home town or neighbourhood is rather short on like-minded individuals I can find on-line communities that share my world view, and in which it will be repeatedly affirmed and valorised.

This relates to spirituality in that, cut free of religious institutions and norms, the spiritual seeker is able to build their own model of belief. Why I wish to characterise this type of self-made faith as 'lite' is in the failure of it to make demands of us, and the way that we are able to jettison aspects that we come to find uncomfortable.

In conventional religion, once you accept its fundamental tenets, you are challenged in two primary ways. Firstly, there may be beliefs, or doctrinal notions, that you find hard to believe. You cannot abandon them though, and have to enter into a reflective, thoughtful, possibly hermeneutic process to try and make sense of them. This is intellectually and personally demanding. It challenges you to take propositional statements, doctrinal beliefs, as serious and worthy of engaging with, no matter how painful and challenging that engagement becomes. Secondly, mainstream religion tells you what to do. This can be seen as negative, and certainly fits with widespread views of religion as a means of social control. But another perspective, not denying the potential for such a usage, is that religion demands that we resist, or at least seek to resist, our most selfish desires. If we follow a religious faith, with sincerity, we are challenged to do some very difficult ethical work[32]: to put others first; to love enemies; to forgive those who do wrong; to cultivate humility. While many will readily admit of their failure in these tasks, and that plenty of believers are insincere and happy to simulate compliance, for someone who takes their beliefs seriously this is a central aspect of the religious life. The ethical challenge of faith demands that we strive to a model of character that does not let us off the hook when it matters. Whatever we think of this, and there are times that, despite my atheism, I find the challenge of religious ethics exceptionally moving and inspirational, it is clear that a 'spiritual but not religious' life makes no such demand. In being adaptable, customisable and flexible we can choose to let ourselves off the hook if we find the ethical demands too much. This may not be in a conscious or insincere manner, but it is clear that the levels of demand in both one's beliefs and actions are substantively lessened in the world of Mind, Body & Spirit. It may replicate some of the features of faith traditions, but non-religious contemporary spirituality is very much a lightened version, shorn of key features found in the full-fat version.

Spirituality and the New Atheism

Since Richard Dawkins' *The God Delusion*[33], it seems like the talk in the virtual and fleshy public spheres has been dominated by an interaction by two ever more shouty choruses. Gathered on one side, we have the serried ranks of atheists and their long-standing sub-corp of the collectively minded known as humanists. Across a chasm of mutual, wilful misapprehension from them are gathered the (largely Christian) hosts of Theism's defenders. I want to suggest here that this debate has become ever more futile, distracting and shrill. Given the largely nihilistic tone of my existential world view, one might expect me to stand shoulder-to-shoulder with Dawkins, Dennett, et al – and I have felt that draw. However the polarising, simplifying nature of the arguments rehearsed leaves, I believe, a substantive middle ground untouched. Further, both sides are ever-more prone to treating religious faith merely as a matter of correspondence-theory metaphysics. Colleagues will know, and readers can surmise in safety, that I am not the world's greatest fan of Theology – but it's as if the discipline has never existed. You'd never know that reflective, intelligent, humane and critical people had actually given the nature and content of religion some sustained and rigorous inspection already.

In trying to articulate this with my students – who often feel draw to one or other of the positions above – I always find myself thrown back on a philosopher I used to consider passé and annoying: Søren Kierkegaard. I will paraphrase him roughly, hopefully driving readers into the arms of his beguiling prose. The key insight that I take from Kierkegaard is his rejection of, and hostility to, the view that religious faith is a rational undertaking – to be defended or assailed via a series of propositional manoeuvres.

In the aftermath of the European Enlightenment of the 18th Century, the idea of the primacy of logic and reason has begun to deeply permeate even the religious institutions it was so often used to criticise. The view exists that (blind) faith is the recourse of the ignorant and unthinking – while the man or woman of thought and reflection accepts or rejects all beliefs (including religious ones – all beliefs are seen as of the same order) on the basis of the evidence for or against them – that is, they are reasonable – requiring a fulfilment of an epistemic duty.

If one accepts this as the ground rules for debating the veracity of religious faith, we can see where it leads – to the need to prove/disprove religious claims – and also we can see how much it seems to look like the current discursive landscape. Kierkegaard has more sense; he's called the father of Existentialism for a reason – and he starts with religion as an engagement with existential realities: doubt, fear, uncertainty and despair. He also wants to challenge the notion that being reasonable is the challenging intellectual position – whereas the person of faith has it easy – being too lazy to think, they just accept what they are told. His view is that it's all very well going around only believing things you have evidence for – that requires no commitment from the thinker: try believing something *without* evidence. Really believing it – not in the lazy way I just mentioned – but actually basing your life on something which you are not only currently unable to prove – but which you know to be unprovable. The 'leap of faith'[34] that this demands, once we really appreciate how serious and life-changing it is, and the intellectual bravery it requires, should make us reconsider the new atheism debate altogether. It should teach us at the very least that the 'creation-science' brigade, the rational defenders of liberal Anglicanism, the 'militant' atheists, and the proponents of new-age crystal twonkery as underpinned by 'quantum science' all share one feature: they miss the central point of what religion even *is*, never mind where we might start a discussion of its benefits and dangers.

This does not mean that I oppose atheism; far from it. It just means shifting the grounds of our rejection. I would argue, but be assured I won't be doing it at length here, for a Nietzschean rejection of a dead God, on the grounds of the existential consequences of the beliefs: you can take your ontological, teleological and cosmological arguments home – they're intellectual playthings and they don't impact on my lived experience.

Given all that, it seems such a shame to see so much energy expended. Many of those on the sceptical and atheist side of this debate (plus a surprising number of the theologically inclined) are strongly opposed to the discourses of spirituality that I wish to critique here – but a mere attack via their rational grounds for belief seems doomed and misguided. They fight the good fight, but can't hope to win: attachment to notions of spirit are not moored in rationality – cutting those bonds leaves belief tethered to culture, emotion and radical fear of death

Over-enthusiastically embracing the new atheism may blind us to the many ways that traditional religion might turn out to be an intellectual ally against the laziness of thought and ethical disengagement of the spirituality-movement. Many traditions *within* formal religions have sought to dispute certain forms of mysticism and Gnosticism – and recognised the threat it represents, not only to their doctrinal dogmas (as it is often portrayed) but also to the efficacy of religions as a means of socio-existential engagement. I will not fully rehearse here the ways that theologians have sought to refute mystic traditions, but what I think is important is to identify a particular thread of discursive posturing that typifies the Spirituality movement's own account of mysticism.

The Perennial Philosophy: Generations of Whine.

At the heart of so much material about contemporary spirituality is that attempt to style it as post-conflict – as syncretic and holistic: it fosters a narrative which concentrates on what we share. Who could argue with that? You can see a physical manifestation of this in new-age centres. Our local one hosts sessions from groups who ought – if taken in some literal or metaphysical way – be at each other's throats. They surely can't all be true at once? But this is where the mystic thesis is introduced as post-rational palliative. The idea of all religions being reconcilable into a single approach was not unknown in the ancient world, and the idea of *Perennial Philosophy* long pre-dates Aldous Huxley's famous book of that title. Nonetheless, it is Huxley who re-articulated the notion in a manner that frames much thinking in contemporary spirituality.

It is an argument we have all absorbed, because it is common currency in the public imagination, although at its strongest in neo-Pagan and similar contexts. Given its all-pervasive nature, I will be as rough in my account as I was in my treatment of Kierkegaard, and rely on the experience of the reader to add their own examples. I fear that this will be all too easy a task. The argument runs something like this:

All religions are borne from the same type of existential encounter something 'beyond.'[35] The founders of faith use analogy and metaphor to communicate this ineffable experience. Furthermore, the key feature of the experience is one of unity – that what seems many is in fact one. While some of the followers of the founder 'get it', many do not[36] – and we then witness the process of the institutionalisation of faith: metaphor becomes taken as literal truth and exclusivism enters the tradition. This leads to the conflict of faith traditions with which we are all too familiar. However – within each tradition are those who recognise the true message – of an experience-able oneness. These however represent a threat to the established order and power within religions – breaking down barriers, and destabilising doctrines – threatening the religion as an institution. The mystic, or would-be-mystic, then points to the suppression and marginalisation of mystical traditions within mainstream religions, and the historical eradication of traditions which they assert as sympathetic to mysticism. [37] Their view often borders on conspiracy theory – there is a network across religions who know the 'truth' of mystical oneness – but on all sides they are assailed by the forces of exclusivist, patriarchal[38], anti-mystic forces. It is a compelling and intoxicating narrative[39] – it explains religious diversity and conflict, while retaining room for a world-transcending belief structure. It also pulls in the temptations of much conspiracy theory – the idea that the *real* history of things is a story lurking beneath the apparent version, which all others – more or less – accept. But you know better – you are not taken in – you stand at the current vanguard of a long line of people who 'thought different' and saw what lay beneath –the truth that would obliterate conflict and unite us all – if only 'they' would let it.

Is this familiar? It sits beneath much new-age, neo-pagan, Mind-Body-&-Spirit thought as intellectual superstructure. The reason I discuss it here is due to the fact that so much of the 'new' atheism entirely neglects this as a target of its concerns, and the most thorough critique of mysticism – of the basis of so much 'contemporary spirituality' comes not from the non-religious but from within traditions themselves. They see it for what it is – a pantheistic monism whose end point, whose logical conclusion, is the stripping away of religious content – leaving only that which cannot be said.

If religions have cared about actual truth, about social justice, and about actually supporting the lived experience of followers with an engaged approach to the realities of being alive, they have opposed mysticism. If those drawn to atheism think this through – they should see a need here to draw on the resources of theology in dealing with the pervasive and insidious threat that spirituality-discourses represent. To the atheist, the pantheistic, mystical monism of the Spirit is worse than a thousand theologians – it threatens to become a moving target, assumed to be true in a way that religious faith can only dream of – and offers to maintain much of what is negative in religion, while jettisoning much of value – like concerns for truth, social justice and engaged living.

If those currently wasting their, and our, time defending theistic claims against Dawkins et al had more sense –they would shift their efforts to targeting the dangers closer to home. The mystic represents a threat to the actual achievement s of religious traditions which is far more dangerous than any atheist – threatening to rot it from the inside, leaving a hollow shell of ineffable nothing.

Chapter Two

The Ancient Wisdom of Post-Modernism
The Authenticity Fetish

Whenever I peruse a new-age catalogue, or browse a publisher's new-book list for Mind, Body and Spirit, I am struck by a particular repetitive fetish. This can be characterised as the fetish of authenticity. This is not particular to new-age spirituality, and can be readily recognised throughout contemporary Western cultures. Slavoj Žižek has made some reference to this, typically scattered across his *oeuvre*[40], and I would assert that it is pervasive. In a world where we are in fear of being fobbed off with a fake or simulated experience, we value the 'real' version hugely. People will tell you that they want to visit the 'real' Spain, to indicate their distaste for the 'Blackpool on the Med', that they are aware of and will avoid the 'tourist version'. This might be seen as the driver for the explosion in amateur pornography (so high is demand, that professional studies have to fake 'amateur scenes'), where the idea that a participants reactions and expressions are 'genuine' and not simulated has high re-sale value.[41]

There are a number of ways this fetish is manifested in our particular context of concerns. Some are obvious, if often disturbing if deconstructed. An easy example: if you are seeking a Yoga teacher, and see two cards on the Post Office noticeboard, one for Krishnan and one for Kevin, you can easily imagine who gets the most enquiries. But beyond such crude, possibly racist, concerns with getting the 'real thing', not some manufactured version, how do we find concerns with authenticity as central, defining, features of contemporary spirituality? These features historically bookend the new-age movement, but are not unknown in mainstream faiths – most notable when it seeks to fly the 'contemporary spirituality' flag. They are the invocation of ancient-wisdom, and of contemporary, or even emergent or future, scientific progress.

Ancient Wisdom

No matter how much new-age thought is portrayed as new, or innovative, or mirroring new discoveries in science, there is almost always a desire to derive a veneer of that most valuable cultural commodity, authenticity, via the invoking of 'ancient wisdom'. Often this is styled in relation to a forgotten wisdom, or (to recall the approach of the mystics we saw earlier) suppressed tradition. While there are instances where the ancient, long-dormant, underground wisdom derives from western traditions (pagan or Celtic, maybe), it is not uncommon for there to be a very specific and distinctive Orientalist twist to the discourse.

In this socio-historical narrative, the West has, in its headlong and frantic rush into the acquisition of mechanistic under-standing, in its development of 'intelligence', lost something along the way. In the 'East', however, they have been less reckless with their mystic legacy and have kept true to ancient ways, not obliterating them underfoot in the name of progress. They may not have developed the 'intelligence' of Western science, and that leads to progress, but they have offset this cost with the benefit of retaining 'wisdom'. Of course this plainly has the potential to slip from crude, generalising ignorance into all kinds of essentialism and racism, but what strikes me most is how familiar it is. Further, this distinction is still widespread in New Age and Mind, Body & Spirit literature, advertising and discussion. This Orientalist, historical, clunkingly bifucatory, narrative was deeply embedded in our culture as part of a Victorian exoticism, and really seems to have stuck. You might argue that it would not have been so stubborn, were there not some truth in it. Maybe Western cultures have, in automating so much, in chasing wealth and efficiency lost vital sight of humanistic values – but I would suggest that we can find critiques of capitalism without the need to invoke 'wisdom', and without the need to patronise other cultural and intellectual traditions. I would suggest that the longevity of the stereotypical account outlined here is due to two key factors. Firstly, it has narrative strength; it is a good story, with a veneer of explanatory power: this makes it compelling and easy to believe. Secondly, rather than being a form of resistance to capitalist alienation and dehumanisation, it actually dovetails with it all too well. If we accept the account that we have let wisdom slip from our grasp, and that this is a phenomena across Western cultures, from San Francisco to Sunderland, and beyond then what we have is a huge market niche. As with advertising, a narrative here creates both the problem and the solution: we have lost our ancient wisdom, but fear not. Some have maintained it elsewhere, or rediscovered it here, and they can sell it to you.

The problem is an alienated society, where community is undermined, where humanistic values are disregarded for profit and greed: and the new age and MSB discourse offers us, as an answer: shopping. While post-modernists may enjoy the irony of this, it seems rather like a sick joke to me.

'As science is now realising...'

Given the widespread disregard for the way science operates, and the regular condemnation of other aspects of the rationalistic (or to use a term often deployed as though pejorative by both new-age writers and contemporary members of mainstream Theistic traditions – 'reductionist') world view that science relies on, there is a lot of new age material which mirrors scientific discourse. Further, there is the claim that science is 'finally catching up with what mystics have long known'.[42] The realm of spirituality is awash with this. Be it the endless volumes on Quantum Consciousness, or Capra's 1975 'Classic' The Tao of

Physics, or the harnessing of biological evolution and attempts to 'spiritualise' it[43], all this material seems exceptionally keen, almost desperate, to associate itself with the idea of science and the very progress which it sometimes laments the consequences, or nature of.

The association with, and invocation of, scientific ideas and terminology is not limited to the new-age, Mind, Body & Spirit setting, but is also found in much contemporary material from more mainstream religious traditions. Further to this, there have long been traditions within, for example, Christianity, Islam and Hinduism, that have sought to demonstrate the compatibility of scientific discovery and the revealed, or inspired, truths of religion. So is the use of science in the discourses of contemporary spirituality merely a continuation of this, or something more? The deployment of the idea of science in contemporary spirituality is distinctive in two key ways – the latter of which is by far the most important. The first, merely annoying, distinctive feature is that way in which Mind, Body and Spirit science-talk always seems to suggest that science is persistently lagging behind their insights, in the unfolding of a progress they often critique. Given their penchant for ancient wisdom, and that what science is 'only now learning' was 'known all along' by the Ancients/East it is tempting to ask why life in the time of ancient wisdom was so unremittingly awful for the great mass of humanity? I would have rather had penicillin than an account of the universe as intricately interconnected and the subtle, provisional nature of matter, but maybe that's just me.

The more disturbing feature of this appropriation of science is that for the consumers, and there are many, of the Mind, Body & Spirit world's publications, TV shows, endless MBS Fairs in town halls and web-sites and tweets, science becomes tainted with what I wish to characterise as a toxic approach to the nature of truth.

Spirituality, Post-modernism and truth

I want to invoke Postmodernism here, because it is via the notion of 'truth' that New Age, Mind, Body & Spirit-led accounts of spirituality and postmodernism largely intersect and coincide. One of the key, identifiable features of postmodernism is its suspicion of grand-narrative-derived accounts of objectivity and truth. Instead, postmodern writers have often offered, on occasion very powerful, accounts of the role of social, intellectual, historical and sexual factors in the construction of what is given as 'truth'. Perhaps most pertinent here is Thomas Kuhn's *The Structure of Scientific Revolutions* (1962) which makes a compelling case for scientific progress as not linear and objective, but as episodic and in a relationship to history and society. His concept of *paradigm shift* is powerful and he argues well for it, grounding his proposition in the detail of the history of science.

Before going further I wish to establish a distinction between much academic work which is labelled as 'postmodern', and its popular representation and consequences. Kuhn offers a philosophically and empirically grounded account of great power; but this, and the work of others, has bled into popular culture as the idea that 'truth is relative'. There is a populist, widely distributed iteration of postmodernism that has certain key features, often occluding the more beneficial insights found in its more scholarly roots. These are the over-stressing of postmodernism as to do with things that were originally only its stylistic container: playfulness, irony, distance and pastiche. Further, the postmodern instinct to reassess ideas of high and low culture, arguably much overdue and necessary to overturn elitist power-structure in society, has in the populist version turned into a collapsing of such distinctions, and the notion that truth is not only multiple, but, vitally, that all attempts to offer an account of truth are of equal value – and that it is elitist to rule out any means for asserting 'truths'.

This non-exclusivist approach to truth is what we find at the intersection of postmodernism and contemporary spirituality. If even science is social construction, there is no meta-narrative for judging between truth claims; without a 'God's-eye view' how can I ever criticise an alternative epistemic methodology? On the ground, this might be best embodied by the way in which a centre for MBS activity hosts events which seem to, on logical grounds, conflict entirely in their accounts of how the universe operates, and what kind of laws are at play. Furthermore, the audience for these events, those who participate, may well practice across the portfolio of offerings – without any sense of conflict.

Of course, one could point to other intellectual antecedents for this epistemic promiscuity. One might look to the Hindu tradition, and to the oft-cited verses of the *Bhagavad-Gita* that seem to suggest that there are many paths to the Ultimate. Perhaps the most famous, and often used, piece of scripture to support such a view is to be found in the Bhagavad-Gita, when Vishnu, in the Avatar of Krishna says to Arjuna:

[Yet] even those who worship other gods with love (bhakta)
And sacrifice to them, full filled with faith,
Do really worship Me,
Though the rite differ from the norm.
For it is I who of all acts of sacrifice
Am Recipient and Lord,
But they do not know Me as I really am,
And so they fall [back into the world of men].[44]

Alternatively, one might follow the Buddha and refer to the blind-men and the elephant.[45] These very examples are, of course, cited widely in the canon of contemporary spirituality. What references to them often miss, though, is that Hinduism partnered its doctrinal flexibility with the imposition of a kind of role-dependent orthopraxy (via *varnasramadharma*), and that the blind men are there not only to point out how different accounts of truth proliferate, but also to provide an analogy that foresees a sighted person – a seer indeed – who sees the whole elephant (the Buddha would be implying that he is the one who sees the whole picture, his competitors being the blind men). The ancient sources of wisdom may seem to support a plurality of truths, but on closer inspection this is clearly just not true. Hinduism requires social cohesion and compliance that would violate the egalitarian sensibilities of most Western 'spiritual seekers', and Buddhism is remarkably more exclusivist and missionary that many are quick to admit.

Once we have ruled out these ancient sources, the populist postmodernist account of truth seems to fit all the more accurately with the approach of new-age, MBS spirituality. What seems to intensify this assault on the notion of the exclusivity of truth (that accepting one truth implies, of necessity, that other truth-candidates that contradict it cannot be also true[46]) is a misreading of liberal, well intentioned, accounts at social inclusivity being over-extended in terms of remit. Accepting that other have different views, which contradict mine, and that we can live together peaceably amidst such disagreement is a good thing. However, assenting to this proposition (which is, alas, a little more messy and complicated than I portray it) does not imply that both accounts views can be true, despite being conflicting. Nonetheless, such presumptions, that all truths have to be seen as simultaneously true, can proliferate as a result of the historical intersection of postmodernist accounts of truth coinciding with political engagements with multiculturalism. We need to robustly contest the idea that just because we have genuine concerns about science's nature as featuring element of social construction, or that we recognise much of Kuhn's critique, that this means that all truth claims are of all value.

This is the toxic account of truth that lies at the heart of contemporary spirituality. By accepting multiple, simultaneously valid truths we abandon the actual meaning of the word 'true'. More importantly, we abandon the struggle to find truth amidst a welter of claims. If we just accept that reiki, tai-chi, rolfing, neo-paganism, and crystal therapy are all equally valid, then we don't have to get our hands dirty wrangling with the mucky detail of their claims. This may be a relief, as disentangling truth claims, the assumptions underlying them, and their unforeseen implications, is hard work. It is what, in the empirical realm, scientists do; in the social, sociologists toil at this work; and philosophers take up the labour-intensive task for existential, metaphysical and epistemological claims. Sorting out what is and isn't true, and what can and can't be, dependent on what we do and don't accept, is vital – and it is hard. I want to be clear here: contemporary spirituality, with its approach to multiple truths, encourages lazy thinking that has a disregard for truth. In this respect it might be seen to be in alliance with a particular manifestation of Postmodernism as a cultural trend. This disregard blinds us to the detail of scientific method, makes us less competent at assessing truth claims from other realms, and undermines rigorous and fruitful debate.

The New-Age Movement: A Road Map to Behind You

Having addressed problematic notions of truth in contemporary spirituality, I want to turn my attention to the more specific detail of certain, intertwined discourses in contemporary spirituality that further accentuate the problems I have set out thus far. A reasonable, well-grounded suspicion of grand meta-narratives should not blind us to the incremental dangers of accumulated micro-narratives.

The three micro-narratives that I wish to look at are those of neo-paganism, eco-spirituality and 'goddess-feminism'. There is a lot more that I could say about each than I will here, because I want to concentrate on how they connect, and how they seem to engender unpalatable implications.

I would like to begin by asserting that are there, in the UK, Europe and USA, today, no pagans at all. Furthermore, it is not clear if any group historically ever self-understood via this term. Whether we can even usefully talk about paganism as a tradition is unclear even to experts in the field, and few in the study of religion use it. More likely it, at best, can be used as an umbrella term for a whole mess of competing and oft incompatible religious approaches, with the only possible common feature being polytheism. The definition of pagan is usually a linguistic category which does not describe in terms of content, but rather in terms of negativity. Those who were not part of some named group become collectively referred to as pagans – occluding their actual traditions and beliefs, and conflating it on the grounds of what it is not.

One feature that clearly persists, then, in what we might best refer to as neo-paganism[47], is conflation. Contemporary neo-pagans see their approach as a spiritual expression integrating witchcraft (expressed often as Wicca), Celtic faith (especially via the idea of Druidism), pan-religious mysticism, with sometime invocation of Norse or other historical pantheons of Deities. Being polytheistic, this is hardly problematic: there are many gods, described in many ways in different places and times. The question of whether individual gods, who are treated as existing by practitioners, actually do exist, or act as metaphors for human intent or psychological traits, is seen by some inside the community as embodying a category mistake – for all three are the case. There is a tone of liberal, friendly inclusivity in neo-paganism that would, one imagines, balk somewhat at the idea that one surely can only believe in these beings metaphorically *or* literally and that the latter would require a drastic process of pruning/selection. However, I don't want to offer here a full critique of neo-paganism. My point here is to merely illustrate that what is actually true is almost irrelevant to the symbolic invocation of deity within neo-paganism, and that this tallies with our account of truth in such spiritualities.

Moving on, I want to look at intertwined discourses that emerge from, at least substantially populate, neo-pagan thought. It is worth noting, however, that these have also been hugely influential in both the wider Mind, Body & Spirit movement, and within both scholarly and popular accounts of more mainstream religions. These are the notions of the environment as being, in some sense, divine; and of the idea of feminine divinity as embodied in the idea of the Goddess. The two are usually described thus that they are intrinsically connected: Goddess spirituality *is* nature-based spirituality for many believers/sympathisers. It is often presented in the context that a male-God-based religion of transcendence has been implicated in a logic of penetration which has raped the earth. I paraphrase, but this is not an unusual neo-pagan claim, the idea of a holistic, unified, nature-based, nurturing spirituality has a clear appeal.

Many quasi-feminist positions within new-age cultures are notable for their reliance on the embodiment of women. Women's bodies are often seen as the site from which anti-patriarchal views arise; as though the previous suppression of women's embodied nature is because of something intrinsic abut them. This often manifests in a variant of Cartesian mind-body dualism; where mind/maleness has been privileged and body/femaleness has been subjugated. There may well be grounds for accepting this as an account of historical associa-tions. However, this association of male as logical, and female as bodily is not only problematic for its privileging of the former: reversing it will not solve the problems here. What we should rather contest is a deterministic relationship between the nature of female bodies and the content of either what it is to be a woman, or feminist thought. Indeed there would appear to be very good reasons for rejecting a male=mind, female=body dualistic essentialism[48], as a form of foundational sexist myth.

Clearly the female body is at the heart of feminist thought, for the ways in which it is proscribed and controlled, but that does not mean that we need to derive from this an essentialist account whereby the content of feminists mind are merely an epiphenomena of their possession of certain biological equipment. As Laurie Penny notes:

At the very heart of sexist thought is the notion that the bodies we are born with ought to dictate our character, our behaviour, our appearance, our choices, the nature of our relationships, and the work of our lives. Feminism puts forward the still-radical notion that this is not the case. [49]

It is worth noting that Goddess worship, and some kind of nature-based monism, truly are ancient beliefs. Feminine accounts of divinity are widespread in the historical world, retaining particular strength in part of South Indian Hinduism. While Spinoza is usually the poster-boy for Western monism, there are versions around the world – though they often have distinctive features of their own that prevent me from describing them as wholly equivalent to each other. How do these features manifest in contemporary spirituality, particularly within neo-paganism?

Clearly an affiliation with the environmental movement is a key feature, a reverence for the natural world. But while loving the planet is a central neo-pagan theme – but does it possess any moral content? That is, is all is the manifestation of the Goddess and her fecundity, what are we called to do? To defend the natural may seem obvious, but are we, the potential rapist of nature, not also part of this natural, poured forth, order? What is usually sought it some form of harmony, of living alongside the natural world in a sustainable way. It is worth noting that while historically neo-paganism may have been part of small, discordant, collection of voices in this matter, it is a message now that the whole choir sings: aren't we all singing from the same hymnbook on that one? Also, when we examine this discourse in more detail, slightly more troubling concerns seem to emerge.

Most religious traditions place humanity in a unique, or privileged position, but if we take much of neo-paganism at face value, that evaporates. We may consider this as a good thing, but contrast it to the Theistic account whereby God takes a personal interest in you. Jesus may love you, but the Goddess probably thinks you are a virus. If we see all life as sacred, surely no life is? For in that context, sacredness means nothing. For some things to be exceptional, special, non-mundane; there needs to be the normal, the mundane and unexceptional. But if all has equal value, then are we not in a world of equivalence where utilitarian cost/benefit calculations are entirely appropriate? On these grounds, might not humans be a major system failure for the Gaia[50] goddess, a skin rash soon to healed via an organic poultice?

Feminist discourses of spirituality walk a troubled line between gender essentialism (women and the earth, as connected, spiritual beings, where gender determines a spiritual inflection of authenticity) and fear. The fear is the real fear – the dread spectre of true mortality and meaningless that rejection of religion seems to represent. There is something rather distressing about discourses of feminist spirituality. It seems to partly acknowledge that patriarchy is rooted in gender determinism, but rather than assert a liberative agenda which allows for self-creation, there is a faintly wistful retreat into an amended essence. Decorating your intellectual prison with leaves, twigs, berries and menstrual blood does not change its underlying purpose.

Further, the pantheistic nature-worship in much Goddess and neo-pagan thought is oddly anti-ethical. It does not enhance our choices with an urgent relational content, but reduces us, in a wider view, to mere bugs on a ball of shit. To be at one with the natural world may have strong ecological credentials, but we need to exceed that world to be ethical. Yes, we are part of the wider natural world, and that connection can be deep and powerful, but we act in bad-faith when we would obliterate or deny our ability to transcend it. We might even argue that the true natural place in the eco-system of humans is most profoundly expressed when we choose not to act like animals.

Just Do It? Why Thinking Matters

Don't think – just act. Says the martial arts teacher. I am thirteen years old, in a *Gi* which is too big for me, and at an Aikido class in a sweat-drenched Leicester gym. I think about what he means, but know that this is the wrong reaction. Distracted by thinking, my back slams heavily into the blue mats.

To 'do without thinking' is a widespread trope of what we might call embodied knowing – be it the climber making a bold or tricky move, blocking the fear and the doubt; or the musician approaching a tricky section of a performance, letting the drive of the music carry them; we know the discourse of 'flow' very well in the West (though suspect we may have acquired it during cultural incursions into the East). For this we are largely indebted to Mihaly Csikszentmihalyi, whose 1990 book *Flow: The Psychology of Optimal Experience* remains influential. On re-reading the book, it becomes harder and harder to be as severely critical (as I had intended to be, from my memory of the book, and more of its influence). There are two key reasons for this, the first of which is the phenomenological explanatory efficacy of his writing. He describes 'flow' in such a way as to make it appear familiar to us: like it was always there, but we never quite saw it for what it was before. The second compelling feature of Csikszentmihalyi's work is the blend of enthusiasm and detail he marshals when advancing his view. My memories of his work, it turned out, were not of it at all, but of the uncritical, un-nuanced and derivative deployments of the idea of 'flow' which we now hear so often. It seems that his care and attention has been swept aside, as it were, by a populist and simplified conception, that does his work a disservice.

This meme of 'flow', of being 'in the zone' has become culturally ubiquitous. You know an idea has had effective cultural dissemination when football players talk about it in post-match interviews. Sports coaches are very keen on the idea, as are other forms of activity where 'performance' is important (such as the pianist example). What I am curious about is how the notion of 'flow' and 'no-thought' adds to the widespread idea we call 'concentration'? It seems to take an idea we know quite well, and are quite adept at generating, and gives it a new-age, spiritual sheen. Maybe we should relax and just think of it as a rebrand? However I think that the idea of non-thinking flow doesn't just not add to concentration as an idea, but rather subtracts something important from it.

Concentration is not to be opposed to thought *per se*. I would argue that it is a particular type of thinking. Now, if we wish to contrast it with other types of thought, this seems to make a certain amount of good sense. Absorbed concentration is how you do maths, as well as how you enact a performance of the body, and it *is* qualitatively different to letting one's mind wander, or other types of mental activity. When the Aikido teacher told me not to think, what he intends is that I stop thinking in a certain way – in an anxious, performance-under-mining self-reflective, self-conscious way, and enter into the activity through an act of concentrated thought. The idea of a typology of thought, and an evaluative engagement with these types, is hardly radical. It is best illustrated, historically, in the *abhidhammapiA aka* of the Pali Canon, the textual tradition of early, ad Theravada, Buddhism. Within this, the Dhammasangani texts illustrate attempts to classify thought in a manner which, although incomplete, makes contemporary colloquialisms about 'head and heart' thinking look like the embarrassing nonsense they are. Mental absorption is clearly delineated in these texts[51] as a type of thinking, something when our brain is very much engaged.

A Zen Digression

Not all forms of Buddhism retain the *abhidhamma* approach to thought. Most notably, that group of traditions much favoured by the new-age (partly due to historical factors in American history, rather than for purely conceptual reasons), Zen Buddhism does seem to oppose thought in many ways. Its use of *koans* to break your ability to think in a logical, conceptual manner seems to rather mirror the anti-thinking strain of contemporary spirituality. It is possible that one could find such an approach in some Zen, ancient and modern, but one could also read it differently. One might, although I do not intend to follow this down the rabbit hole of Zen[52], suggest that the mind-breaking power of *koans*[53] is not to leave us, ultimately, with a mind free from all thought, which then merely sees the world as it is. Once the work of the *koan* is done, the mind is like a blasted landscape, which is not abandoned, but repopulated with a radically different thought process; one free from the 'taints' that obscure the clarity of vision that Zen aspires to, and that the best Zen *haiku*[54] can give us a glimpse of. Although I would have to go some way to convince many Buddhism scholars, and further with some practitioners, I would still maintain that much Buddhism, shorn of certain spiritual accretions and maybe even some of its ancient roots, represents a system for re-thinking thought.

Flow and Thought: Thinking as craft practice

What should we take from this discussion? Why does my hostility to this discourse of 'flow' and 'no thought' matter? I would argue that it is part of the disabling of thought brought about spirituality. By disaggregating the human into these discrete sections – mind, body and spirit; head and heart, there is a lazy and pernicious simplification at work. If we merely need to 'go with the flow of our heart', or 'harken to the quiet, little voice of the inner spirit' – then we enter a realm beyond disputation. If, however, our reflective, contemplative activity; even our embodied mind-body engagement in activity, if all these are forms of thought – then we have two substantive, genuine benefits to be harvested from the rejection of the proto-spiritual annexing of them. First of these is that we can question them, critique them and open our contemplation to rigour and demand it rises to meet dialogical challenges. Secondly, if we conceptualise these activities as varieties of thinking, we can improve them – we can do more than merely listen, or just allow the flow to flow. As agents of our own thoughts, we can render a model of thinking as a craft practice. Even if we still wish to keep the idea of 'flow' because we believe it has a powerful phenomenological resonance, we improve it conceptually by considering that it is our own efforts that sculpt the pathways of such flowings.

In this, as in much else, we need to cling with a certain ferocity, to concepts that deliver to us our own responsibility. Outsourcing mental activities into a realm of 'no thought' moves them further from our ability to choose, from our agency. This plays into a fatalistic discourse, where we are merely along for the ride, and where resisting the flow is 'unhealthy'. As I will outline in the next chapter, this has consequences beyond merely allowing us to turn off our own critical and reflective capacities for thought in a personal sense.

From Science to Spirit: Why Truth Matters

I don't direct this critique merely at obviously fraudulent/ misguided practices such as homeopathy, and crystal healing, but more widely. Across the spectrum of contemporary spirituality, the question of: "yes, but who is right? Which account of reality has more explanatory and predictive power than others?" is set aside, often in the name of inclusivity or liberal openness. But inclusivity of belief is not belief at all, but a posture of un-truth, of not knowing even what truth is. The seemingly benign world of spiritual syncretism, particularly in the new-age movement, is a blend of arrogance and nervousness. Arrogance regarding somehow have transcended the need for demonstrating the full basis and rationale for beliefs, and nervousness about actually being called upon to do so, especially when having invoked half-understood concepts imported from science or philosophy.

In this chapter, I have argued that there is a model of truth at work in the realm of contemporary spirituality that is actually a refusal to accept an uncomfortable truth about truth. This truth is that truth is intrinsically judgemental, exclusive and difficult. That there are numerous philosophical problems regarding the nature of truth, and these do exist, does not mean that we cede the whole debate to those who believe we can merely choose what to believe on the basis of a lazy, faux-postmodern, neo-liberal inclusivity. It is the case that correspondence theories, scientific coherence models, falsification hypotheses, social constructivist accounts and a wealth of others dispute what truth is, and how it can be understood, determined articulated. Being amongst philosophers, and other academic disciplines, the divisions around these debates are bitter, often long standing and full of vociferous disputation. We should read this as exceptionally healthy. It shows that truth is being taken seriously, that we realise that this actually matters.

We can contrast this to what I believe is the most damning aspect of the attitude to truth taken by much contemporary spirituality: its dismissiveness. All too often challenges to the rational, logical basis of spirituality-claims are waved away, as though to believe in the idea of mutually exclusive accounts of truth is somehow naive and rather conservative. The peaceful co-existence of truth-claims, within spirituality, that ought to be in tenacious dispute, is not evidence of wise toleration and reservation of judgement. Rather it is evidence of an abandonment of critical thought, a stubborn, almost childlike, refusal to choose or judge, and repeated exposure to it blunts the sharpness of our critical faculties. It makes us into idiots.

Chapter Three

The Ghost of the Political
Spirit and Community: A patchy history

One feature of new age practice which has attracted significant comment in academic and popular literature has been the difficulties these traditions have had in fostering any sense of shared community or collective sensibility. [55] One might go as far as proposing that the new-age practitioner is emblematic of a contemporary sense of society which is made up of atomised individuals, each with their own interests, rarely shared by neighbours, connected only by loose, often virtual, networks with the like-minded. These like-minded networks might simulate community, but they do not enact it authentically – they serve to actually draw people away from the people they live among, who serve them in local shops, service their cars, who they walk amidst in their non-virtual, disconnected, fleshy lives. Much 'mind-body-spirit' spirituality seems to hover between the description of 'client cult' and 'audience cult', in the nomenclature developed in Rodney Stark and William Sims Bainbridge's *The Future of Religion: Secularization, revival and cult formation*. They note that commitment to audience cults, in particular is the lack of commitment to a particular idea, and this is a major factor in their failure to bind groups, people and communities in the way that traditional religions have often done. They suggest, before using an audience who had expressed approval of Von Däniken's theory and researching their attitude to other ideas such as astrology and ESP that:

> One of the hallmarks of audience cults is that the typical audience is interested in several of them simultaneously and

does not have a secure faith in any one of them.[56]

This also seems to match much of what we find the world of contemporary, most notably Mind-Body-Spirit, spirituality; although I would suggest that in MBS settings there is a more secure faiths, as members move towards more being a 'client' than an 'audience' member, and their repeated purchasing activity demonstrates repeated acts of faith, and an investment in believing the activities to be efficacious/true. Nonetheless the first point, regarding the promiscuity of belief, holds true and I would suggest is one part of an explanation as to why contemporary spirituality is often so slow or weak when it comes to generating either community or political cohesion.

Serial Objections.

One might object in three key ways to this characterisation, and these objections do have some weight. Firstly, one might make an empirical, historical point, or pair of them. That these communities take time to grow; that early members of other, now community-centric, traditions were initially geographically dispersed thinly. Further, it might be suggested that things have moved on and the movements have bred their own local community networks.

Secondly, there is my rather scurrilous use of 'authentic' above. Why is a virtual community not equally authentic? Cannot it enact behaviour modification on its members, generate norms, and resolve disputes in ways that might be sometimes worse, other times better than the accidental communities of historical, social coincidences of place.

A third complaint might also be introduced, which disputes that community living is that important at all, and refers to the tradition of outsiders as bearers of truth, of the value of the rebel and the one who refuses to accept socially-approved activity, and steps outside the community to critique it. Certain parts of the new-age movement might be rather keen to deploy this third way, pointing to the members it retrospectively annexes (such as witches and herbalists) and their historical, or mythic, exclusion from communities over generations.

One the first point, I would concede that there are places where the growth of those involved in forms of avowedly non-religious spirituality has grown substantially, and even to the extent that one could reasonably claim that a physically-centred community exists. Nonetheless, such places are confined to large cities, with a few notable smaller locations which have become magnets due to their reputations as new-age centres. Probably the most notable is Glastonbury, some parts of the town feeling like a new-age theme park, or perhaps more accurately like a new-age version of an outlet shopping mall. More locally, to me, is Stroud – described to me by colleagues when I moved to the region as the 'Crystal capital of the Cotswolds'.

Despite this reputation, the streets of this town seem fairly similar to any other English town, and you actually need to try hard to spot the shops and clinics in which this reputation is grounded. The size to which new-age, neo-pagan and related communities have grown is hardly comparable to the community penetration of even somewhat, according to some popular perceptions, down-at-heel traditions such as Christianity. To see how few people actually label themselves belonging to a religion outside *the big six* (Buddhism, Judaism, Islam, Hinduism, Christianity and Sikhism) we can look to the 2001 census, where we see it is 0.28%.[57]. Part of the problem derives from the very nature of contemporary spirituality: where membership is not the primary way people conceptualise their involvement. It is perfectly conceivable for someone to engage fully in a 'spirituality', in that they buy mind, body & spirit books, attend yoga, or crystal workshops, and subscribe to RSS feeds regarding their particular profile of spiritual interests – but still feel that they are unable to tick that they 'belong to another religion' on the form: because they don't self-understand their practice, or engagement, as 'religious'. Nonetheless, the census still only returns 7.76% as 'religion not stated', and 15.05% as 'no religion'. Even if all these people were like-minded spiritual seekers, this would still fall under being a quarter of the population: and many of these people clearly are not such individuals. Further it is clear that even when there might be a large number of people who are interested in spiritual matters, they are often far from entirely overlapping. Even where there are greater numbers, communities are fragmented, and patterns of involvement are very much personally constructed, rather than mandated by a specific formula, commitment or pre-existing social norm. The first objection appears to be exceptionally shaky, and we are some way from large local communities of neo-pagans, and the nature of engagement means that huge numbers of participants are casual consumers of this cultural phenomenon that seems almost entirely at odds with even the idea of a community.

The accusation that I use 'authentic' disingenuously seems harder to resist. Who is to say what constitutes an authentic community? From the early, pre-WWW, days on the internet, through IRC forums, to the Social Network explosion, the construction of virtual communities has been an area of vigorous and remarkably human activity. By human, I indicate that contrary to some predictions that computers were going to make us ever more passive recipients of corporation-pumped entertainment, people have seemed to have revealed something noteworthy about ourselves as a species via the way we have shaped the use of global, interactive, computer networks. This revelation was not unknown before, Aristotle noted it[58] as a, possibly the, distinctive feature of humans. It is that people are fascinated by people, and by the act of communication, and by levels of subtlety, wit, nuance, humour, sarcasm, as well as malice, anger and incredulity, requiring a huge expenditure of time and energy. This insight helps explain why people are 'addicted'[59] to social networks; we get to do what humans are really talented at. For these and other reasons, I am happy to acknowledge the possibility, and sometime existence, of virtual communities that deliver in all sorts of ways, the benefits (and often also the drawbacks) of more historical, geographically centred versions. Sometimes, these benefits may well outstrip those of traditional models of community: allowing for a distinct focus, more understood self-referential use of language, and ease of access. Just because I happen to have washed up, due to accidents of personal history, in a particular place – what reason is there to assume that I share commonalities of interest with this accidentally nearby humans? Virtual communities allow me to bridge away from my isolation and laugh, joke, dispute, bicker, and fall in love with fellow-travellers around the globe.

Nonetheless, I still feel that over-reliance on virtual community as a riposte to the accusation that contemporary spirituality is depoliticising, isolating and has the potential to make us selfish and self-regarding is an insufficient response. We can build the communities online that I refer to here – but *where* we live, and who else lives here, really matters. Despite the attempt by party politics to annex it, there is some recognition more broadly in many communities of the values of 'localism', and of the importance of communities engaging with all of their members in constructive ways. Physical and virtual communities are not mutually exclusive, and we don't need to choose, but the idea that we can neglect the former, and rely only on the latter, makes little sense. I write this in the week of the 2011 riots on the streets of many English cities, and am minded to note that any commentator with sense has drawn attention to the concern that too many young people do not feel a sense of integration into their local communities. Living together is a group experience, and while it should clearly be a cradle of diversity as well as of shared concerns, finding ways of connecting to those around us seems more urgent a challenge than ever before. Living together, as a common endeavour, in a physical community in a way that facilitates peaceful, decent lives of mutual respect, demands of us that we look beyond the glowing screen, past our curtains, and live amongst our actual neighbours.

The final objection, of the value of rebellious outsiders, of those who have been the engine of social and ethical progress through their refusal of shared community values, is a serious one. Nonetheless, I do not believe it is a tenable one. Conceptualising the way we have left behind, to the extent that we have, slavery, some of the crasser forms of sexism and racism, more extreme homophobia, child labour and a host of previously accepted behaviours and attitudes is of primary importance. Nonetheless, I would suggest that this has been through people who were very much engaged within communities. They may have been ostracised or excluded as a result of their views, but they were in the world they critiqued. Martin Luther King Jr was not a hermit, a recluse who opted out of society, neither was Nelson Mandela. The abolitionists in the UK, the suffragettes, the founders of Stonewall, these groups were at odds with many in society – but their response is to engage more, not less: to take the challenge to people, to be "in their face" and demand that all change. The alternative is to retreat into private (often virtual) communities, where all share a view, and let the rest of the world do its own thing.

This retreat into the private, a ceding of the public space to merely corporate interest, seems a key feature of much contemporary spirituality: build a paradise in your home, your support networks, your practice, and let the rest of the world find its own way. While this kind of disengagement from the political has political roots, often in a sense of impotence and disenfranchisement, I would posit contemporary spirituality as both symptom and cause of people unplugging from the world of local, regional and national shared sense of togetherness.

The post-ideological world view and the turn to the Self

Alongside post-modernism's suspicion of the grand narratives of ideology, another discourse conspires in contemporary culture, in a strange kinship with much contemporary spirituality, to turn us away from the political, the messy human world of living together in diversity and commonality, towards an ever greater solipsistic self-regard. This is the discourse of the end of history. Famously articulated by Francis Fukuyama in his 1989 essay 'The End of History' and in his later writings, the notion asserts that we have gone beyond competing ideological positions to a time of consensus about politics. It claims that liberal democracy is obviously the superior form of civil organisation, and that what remains now is how to best manage this world, how to manage competing special interests, and facilitate economic growth. That world events since 1989 have demonstrated just how stubbornly history refuses to die has not prevented certain parts of Fukuyama's thinking from penetrating our culture very deeply. We might see a key part of this being the cultural suspicion we have of those deeply committed to ideological positions. The fervent believer (be it in religion, or a political commitment) can seem somewhat antiquated to many. This might be seen to lie at the heart of the 'spiritual, but not religious' pose: "I am deep, but don't worry I am not one of those people who actually believe things so strongly that it leads me to challenge others about life choices, or social structures more widely". If we have a widely distributed social discomfort with the idea of commitment to belief, and prefer an, albeit mythic[60], pragmatic inclusivity, it is worth noting that this pressure to disengage is further exacerbated by key features of spirituality, leading ever inwards, on our self-regarding 'inner journey',

So further to a general sense of party politics as passé and all rather 'twentieth century', what are these other factors? The connection with spirituality is two-fold. Firstly, there is a strong strand of fatalism in much 'spiritual' thinking, which encourages us not to resist, not to be the grit in the machine, but to go with the flow. To move with the cosmic energy, and find the path it would flow us down.

A second factor here is the persistent denial of the reality, or substantiality, of the material world, or its existence in a way consistent with the apparent conclusions of everyday perception. If the world of appearances is just a set of illusions, is just *māyā* then its problems do not *really* matter – furthermore it is unlikely to be the place to find meaning, purpose or satisfaction for your life. In his critique of Western Buddhism, Žižek notes that:

> *if the external reality is ultimately just an ephemeral appearance,*
> *even the most horrifying crimes eventually DO NOT MATTER.* [61]

Alongside this is the persistent fetishisation of poverty, or at least the assertion of the benefits of the simple life. We see this in much conventional religion, and very strongly in new-age traditions. The rejection of 'materialism' is a heady discourse, and there is a good reason for this. Things, material objects, will not make us happy – but the spiritual dialogical two-step here is the trick whereby through a process of bifurcation it is made to seem that *either* we are shallow materialists, seeking bliss in the trinkets of consumerist capitalism, *or* we look deeper to a life of the spirit. It is presented as though a non-spiritual, non-consumerist life of happiness and fulfilment is so impossible, or unthinkable, as to not merit a mention.

Of these, though, the idea of 'fate' or 'destiny' seems both the most intoxicating and persistent. What is perverse is that these discourses about our impotence on a grand, or macro, scale, are often found intertwined with an account that praises 'self-mastery', and a version of the line "we can't fix the world, but we can change ourselves" [62]. When our happiness is rooted in our own behaviour, in our response to an external world over which we believe we have little control, then we lose. We lose the desire to change to world, as we lose the belief that change can happen. Self-mastery is an intoxicating and compelling notion, but to see it as cut adrift from material, most notably socio-economic, realities is to pass true mastery to others.

Me as Brand, Shopping in the Spiritual Supermarket

We become self-obsessed, narcissistic solipsists if we fall for either of twin discourses of the Self. One is that of Self development, the idea that each of us is our own little project – where we dip into the portfolio of inclusivist new-age truth agenda of self-help, as an atomised work of artistry. The other, even more noxious and repellent, discourse is that of people as brands. While this is another area, it is worth noting how spirituality fits here. It is another accessory. Put a Buddha on your mantelpiece to indicate to visitors that you have a spiritual side, that you may be dull and selfish, put you acknowledge a little counter-culture influence. Put your Che Guevara t-shirt on when you go to the shopping mall. The (postmodern) irony will make the sales assistant smile. It will do nothing to help bring about the end of capitalism, but that is a 20th Century naïve dream, from a time of 'history'. The most I can do is to smile wryly and buy another CD that asserts its distaste for personal property (but don't you dare spread that message via per-to-peer file sharing).

Conclusion

Having set out to demonstrate that discourses of spirituality are an engine for depoliticisation, and that they turn us away from others, into a solipsistic self-regard, it may appear that I am against self-improvement. While it is true that I feel that the Western discourse of 'self-development', especially when articulated via spirituality, is malign, and I would include the vast majority of 'life coaching', motivation therapy, and other outsourcing of personal responsibility as part of this; this does not rule out that we might find ways of becoming better people.

As I set out at the start of this chapter, the most effective way to be better people is to be better to people. Ethical self improvement is not something that I can do by myself. Furthermore, it does not need me to buy any paraphernalia, nor to burn any incense, or go on any inner journey. It may be that I *can* deal with my behavioural imperfections through some type of therapy, or use a little mindfulness, but at best this can only be a pragmatic means for engaging with what *really* matters: a more ethical interaction between humans at both micro and macro levels – what we used to call friendship and politics.

Chapter Four

Happiness and the Truth of Death
The Cult of Happiness

It seems as though you can't move at present without encountering happiness. Not the real thing, of course – not an actual experience of joy, or bliss or over-brimming pleasure. No, we're either far too cynical or wise for that. [63] What I mean is a newspaper article or polite conversation: truisms about the need to understand and nurture human happiness are now almost as prevalent as the obnoxious ones about spirituality with which I began this volume. Another proxy for this discourse, imbued with a sheen of medical respectability, is that related to 'wellbeing'. Now, there is something more to the discussion of wellbeing – as an attempt to view physical and mental health in an integrated, holistic[64] context - that I think is useful. It may prove of pragmatic benefit in addressing some of the overly clinical/medicalised aspects of health treatment. However, the problem lies in the elasticity of the term – and its widespread deployment within new age contexts that imply that being holistic in the treatment of humans involves not only mind and body, but also some third element of spirit – and that neglecting it leads to a deficit of wellbeing. Having said all this, I think it best, for our purposes here, to set the term 'wellbeing' to one side –and to get to the heart of the matter: human happiness.

Given that the thrust of this volume is that spirituality's third toxic consequence is that it makes us miserable, surely I am in favour of happiness? The answer is, identical to the one which I use to taunt and annoy my students in classes on Buddhist thought, 'yes and no'. I think we have a potential for full, rich and engaged lives which an approach to life as spiritual endangers – but that still leaves me as exceptionally uncomfortable with the contemporary discourses on happiness which populate the media so fully at present. Before offering my critique, I want to briefly inspect these approaches, lest readers feel I am being overly polemical, or presenting some form of Aunt Sally/Straw Man argument. In an article published in the Guardian in 2001, the British Prime Minister Tony Blair is quoted as being deeply committed to this agenda:

> "It's time we admitted that there's more to life than money and it's time we focused not just on GDP but on GWB – general wellbeing."

Speaking at the Google Zeitgeist Europe conference, he added:

> "Wellbeing can't be measured by money or traded in markets. It's about the beauty of our surroundings, the quality of our culture and, above all, the strength of our relationships. Improving our society's sense of wellbeing is, I believe, the central political challenge of our times."[65]

Strong words. In some ways he can be seen as following Nicolas Sarkozy, and a host of others in seeking to broaden the intent of the politician from economic growth to the fostering of a better quality of life. Read that sentence again. When did the intent of the political ever get reduced to generating the conditions for economic growth anyway? Only in a Fukuyama-inspired, post-ideological, neo-liberal, intellectual wasteland could Cameron's statement even seem to make sense. We do not, however, live in such a world The real obstacles to happiness are just as stubbornly economic, for almost all humans, as they have ever been, and the blend of new-age thought and positive thinking we see in the 'happiness movement' seems like such thin-soup for so meaty a challenge. As Barbara Ehrenreich remarks in her excellent *Smile or Die*, when saying that *once* everyone's basic material needs are met, there will be room for utopia and widespread happiness:

> But we cannot levitate ourselves into that blessed condition by wishing it. We need to brace ourselves for a struggle against terrifying obstacles, both of our own making and imposed by the natural world. And the first step is to recover from the mass delusion that is positive thinking.[66]

This is a compelling reminder of the distance between most humans and the questions that the happiness movement poses to its, largely privileged, first-world audience. Nonetheless, it is worth noting that some of the reflective promoters of this movement are also aware of the problems and criticisms associated with it. In his widely purchased *Happiness: Lessons From a New Science*[67] Richard Layard deals with many of the objections that are often raised: happiness is selfish, it is indefinable, and concerns regarding income and its relation to satisfaction. The book is a mix of open discussion and rather hastily reached conclusion, notable also for its lack of engagement with the issue of human mortality. As a reader interested in all sides of the argument, and genuinely interested in human potential, Layard's book represents something of a high water mark for the happiness movement, with little since which has not been overly tainted by a certain fervour and zeal.

Just as New Age spirituality always seeks to acquire authenticity via an alleged grounding in 'ancient wisdom', the Happiness gurus are also keen to draw on the writers of the past. Most commonly invoked is Aristotle, and his notion that the purpose of life is the acquisition, or manifestation, of *eudemonia*. While the notion of 'human flourishing' (as it is often translated) is not intrinsically problematic, the attendant absence of context can be rather misleading. Ancient Greek philosophy focussed a lot of energy on the question of how to live. It is one thing that distinguishes from the grey, desiccated husk that stands for all too much analytic philosophy. This means that the nature of happiness, and its relationship to both the individual's virtue, and their experience of external factors, was a matter of substantive debate.

When *eudemonia* is used in the contemporary context, however, it seems presented as though it were a unitary notion that we can import to enhance our otherwise shallow, unhappy lives. It was a contested idea – and for good reason. What we tend to find in contemporary characterisations is that a life of human flourishing is one where the concept of happiness resists analysis. The Greeks wrangled over the relationship between happiness and virtue. Look at the books on how to be happy, and there may be some mention of social issues; but what is absent is the insistence that acting in a just and ethical matter is a moral prerequisite for deserving to be happy at all. As Kant might argue, we should not strive to be happy, but seek to deserve happiness. This strikes me as indicative of a peculiar ethical blindness, and a further look at Happiness as a 'movement' does little to improve matters.

The biggest UK happiness advocacy group 'Action for Happiness' offers philosophical antecedents to their views[68], but its prescription is one which reads like a digest of 20th Century Self-help books.[69] Given the previous discussion of science and the new-age, it was interesting to come across this text on the Action for Happiness web-site's home page: 'Western neuroscience has now confirmed what Eastern wisdom has known for a long time: happiness is a skill we can learn'.[70] I am not convinced that this is quite how neuroscientists would put it. Further, haven't some people always known how to be happy? Learning not to care about other people seems quite effective: I am struck here by the 1989 Woody Allen film *Crimes and Misdemeanours*, where the lead character kills his mistress, and after a period of guilt is surprised to note the guilt fades and he is able to carry on with a happy life. Aren't successful, arrogant, uncaring egotists often, actually, quite happy? They may have even acquired their happy lives without the help of ancient wisdom.

While most contemporary happiness movements do blend in a nod towards social justice, and the happiness of others, two things primarily strike me about them. Firstly, it largely comes across as rebranded Utilitarianism[71], and largely disregards the account which integrates the necessity of one's own virtue. The second point, one often at forefront of much Stoic thinking, and which seems to receive too-fleeting a glance from the happiness-movement is the briefness of life and the lack of intrinsic worth or meaning within it.[72] Many of the Stoics seem to pre-empt the European philosophical preoccupation with existential questions, and see happiness as connected to an acceptance of finitude:

No good thing renders its possessor happy, unless his mind is reconciled to the possibility of loss.[73]

Now, to be fair, there *is* an attempt to deal with questions of life's knocks in the happiness movement. This is largely styled around the idea of 'resilience', and the leading figure in Positive Psychology, Martin Seligman, even trialled 'emotional resilience' classes in UK schools in 2007. These were not adopted widely, after inconclusive, and certainly not glowing, research into their impact. [74] Further, these seem to me to not fully appreciate the depth of human anxiety about our mortality, and the finitude of lived experience. What I wish to consider now is what happens if we really want to take seriously questions about death and its impact on our potential to live meaningful lives.

Death and Happiness

Orientating our lives towards happiness, thinking that we could, if only we lived better, somehow achieve it, it so set sail for a false destination. The destination for all lives is the grave, and the spirituality and happiness movements can be seen as the same as hobbies, politics-following as pastime, exercise and health addiction – they are attempts to drive death from the mind – a fundamental denial of death. But what else can we do? Before I look more at the thousand deaths died by those who seek to evade the thought of it, I want to quote T. Z. Lavine, writing about the views of Heidegger:

> If I take death into my life, acknowledge it, and face it squarely, I will free myself from the anxiety of death and the pettiness of life - and only then will I be free to become myself.[75]

Here is not nihilistic pessimism, but a chink of light. But before we fixate on that, it is time to consider what our inner lives are like if we won't rise to the Heideggerian challenge.

The Death of a Thousand Deaths

Sublimated death is never absent. It haunts every attempt at immersing ourselves in life and activity. It is at the bottom of every whisky glass, and reflected in the faces of the children we dote on. In an obsessive home décor frenzy we can never truly forget the rot, stench and decline that will inevitably overrun the matching colours and fabrics. Every outfit I select, revelling in accessorising my vintage discoveries, speaks to the approaching decomposition of the flesh which it covers. And it is not just in things that we can find no refuge. In 'doing', as well as 'having' (to cite a common trope of the happiness movement) we can only mask death, but such that the mask never reaches to the edge of the immensity of our sublimated mortality.[76]

When I run in the woods, I am never alone. I have, at the far edge of my peripheral vision an ever-present companion. No matter how far or fast I run, no matter how loud the music in my ears, or the internal chatter of body-sensing and breath-mastery exercises, I can always seem him. Behind a tree, or glimpsed just protruding from beyond the horizon, the grim figure will not be outrun.

Where does contemporary spirituality fit here? In the new-age, there is a central tenet that death is not the end. This is like a chanted paradox. Nonetheless, repetition, no matter how earnest, will make it into sense. The end is what death is. It is its fullness of meaning. Its end-ness is what inhabits the concept most fully. To repeat the mantra of non-end-ness to death is to stand with eyes closed, fists clenched and to scream against a hurricane. The new age approach is to dwell beneath a duvet of (self)deception and hope that the dawn's fresh light will chase away the demons. The demon of death is not scared of daylight though, and walks proud through our circles of protection; lord of nature, rather than repelled by it.

In the introduction to his book of analytic reflections[77], Ben Bradley quotes Socrates' claim that the task of the philosopher is to prepare for death and to practice for dying. He begins his own text with the claim that "Nobody holds' Socrates view about Philosophy anymore. But death remains a rich source of philosophical questions" [78] I was startled when I read this. I think more and more that this is *exactly* the very task of philosophy – to make meaning in the face of absolute death. This led me back to the source of Bradley's quote – the *Phaedo* – to see what Socrates was really saying and how closely his claim accords to the line of thought I have been developing in this chapter. What I found was that in the *Phaedo*, Plato has Socrates say of the nature of the Philosopher something rather intriguing about death and something that can be read in a very straightforward manner, but that can also put us in mind of a more substantive set of reflections and considerations. Socrates makes the claim that a man who is a philosopher, or who has the spirit of philosophy within him, is willing to die – and a discussion takes place about the relationship of the philosopher to death. Then we encounter the line quoted by Bradley, and many others:

I deem that the true disciple of philosophy is likely to be misunderstood by other men; they do not perceive that he is ever pursuing death and dying[79]

Or in the translation as Bradley cites it:

The one aim of those who practice philosophy in the proper manner is to practice for dying and death.[80]

What we discover if we read on is the view that the philosopher is one who seeks to find what is true and lasting – and while the world of the flesh is changing and unreliable, the world of the soul is the one that accords with permanence and truth. And death is when the soul separates from that which is temporary:

Then, Simmias, as the true philosophers are ever studying death, to them, of all men, death is the least terrible. Look at the matter in this way: how inconsistent of them to have been always enemies of the body, and wanting to have the soul alone, and when this is granted to them, to be trembling and repining; instead of rejoicing at their departing to that place where, when they arrive, they hope to gain that which in life they loved (and this was wisdom), and at the same time to be rid of the company of their enemy. Many a man has been willing to go to the world below in the hope of seeing there an earthly love, or wife, or son, and conversing with them. And will he who is a true lover of wisdom, and is persuaded in like manner that only in the world below he can worthily enjoy her, still repine at death? Will he not depart with joy? Surely he will, my friend, if he be a true philosopher. For he will have a firm conviction that there only, and nowhere else, he can find wisdom in her purity. And if this be true, he would be very absurd, as I was saying, if he were to fear death.

He would, indeed, replied Simmias.

And when you see a man who is repining at the approach of death, is not his reluctance a sufficient proof that he is not a lover of wisdom, but a lover of the body, and probably at the same time a lover of either money or power, or both?

That is very true, he replied.

There is a virtue, Simmias, which is named courage. Is not that a special attribute of the philosopher?

Certainly.

Again, there is temperance. Is not the calm, and control, and disdain of the passions which even the many call temperance, a quality belonging only to those who despise the body and live in philosophy?

That is not to be denied.[81]

So – we can see what the plain reading is of this section – a reading not wholly out of step with neo-Platonic accounts, of course, of contemporary spirituality. We could leave the matter there, and accept Socrates as a proponent of the soul – albeit one a little anti-body for many of those who wish to argue for a holistic account of the mind, body and soul: because it would appear here that the body is of no value – something to be loved by the fool and the common person. But as is usually the case, we lose out if we choose to dismiss Socrates so glibly.

What strikes me on reading this exchange is not a disdain for the body in a dismissive, dualist manner (that we often attribute to a Greek-inspired dualist model of Christian theology) – but rather death as the catalyst for the consideration of the non-worldly. Here we can see death as that which drives us to consider the purpose and meaning of life. Here the non-worldly does not require a leap into the epistemological black hole of metaphysical entities of the spiritual – but rather can indicate the potential of humans to go beyond. 'To go beyond' here is to overcome self-centeredness, to go beyond self-survival, power and wealth - and to believe in the value of others, both individually and via our communal efforts[82]. To the person who achieves that death cannot any longer hold the fullness of dread that it does in a mere, blank for of nihilism. Here, preparation for death is holistically entangled with the journey to discovering the purpose of our own lives. By this means of thought, we can be the philosophers of Socrates' imagination, without the need for the metaphysics of antiquity.

The Strange Case of the Longevity Movement – An Aside

If death provides the impetus for understanding life; once we drag it from behind the Wizard of Oz-like curtains n our mind, it offers us the means to learn who we might be. But what if death really might be indefinitely postponed? Heidegger's three features of death[83] include the absolute inescapability of death, but close behind the growth in 'happiness' features in Sunday newspaper magazines, popular science publications and TV documentaries is the Longevity movement. The general line of thought is that given the prior rate of medical advance, and the prospect of genetic manipulation (especially the idea of an 'ageing gene'[84]), indefinite human lifespans are surely only just around the corner.[85] The Daily reported in 2008 'Why Man COULD Live Forever'[86] and the Independent, in the same year, asked 'Who wants to live for ever? A scientific breakthrough could mean humans live for hundreds of years.' [87] Probably the most notorious advocate of this movement is Aubrey de Grey, with his view that the first humans to live for lifespans of around 1000 years will be born in the next decade or so.[88]

While any detailed examination of the science invoked will

promptly dispel the idea that such an ambitious extension to our lives is likely at all, and even a moment's reflection will generate a host of reasons as to why it may be even less desirable that it is likely, it is still a compelling narrative. Who really wants to die – when they could just keep living? Of course mortality is necessary, and the species needs it – but not for me. Surely my survival, my ever-accumulating wisdom, will be a noble exception, a major benefit to society? We could all advance such self-serving arguments, but if we really take the idea seriously, we have to see it as an attempt to impose stasis on the inevitable flux that is reality, as John Gray recognises:

> Seekers after immortality look for a way out of chaos; but they are part of that chaos, natural or divine. Immortality is only the dimming soul projected on to a blank screen. There is more sunshine in the fall of a leaf.[89]

The longevity movement shares one notable feature with much of the spirituality movement, which is the desire to appear somehow at the very cutting edge of science, but also in some type of tension with 'the establishment' of science. The tone of longevity writers often makes little or no explicit reference to spirituality, although they do often share an interest in the 'holistic', and the idea that somewhere in 'ancient wisdom' secrets may be hidden away. The issue that makes them interesting here, though, is the motivation itself. Given that death *is* inevitable, that mortality and finitude is blindingly and undeniably the frame in which we live our lives – why engage in these grand acts of self-delusion? Of course, some life extension may be possible, but death will not be denied, and, even if delayed a little *en route* by healthy living and medical advances, is coming for us all soon enough. I can only see a single psychological motive underpinning the longevity movement, and this is the same reason it sells newspapers and fascinates so many of us.

This motive is our absolute and total fear and dread. The more we have suppressed death[90], the more we may fail to express our anxiety – but it has gone nowhere. I would contest that underneath the cheery hopes of living for centuries is a screeching, desperate flailing panic at the knowledge of our own, personal, death. The fact of death is, alas, still a fact; and longevity and immortality are as useless as the cheap trinkets of 'heaven' and post-death-life. What little we can do, surely, consists of the staring down, and confronting of the truth of death. This choice promises no escape, but at least offers us the chance to live a life where death's long shadow does not taint every thought via poorly-repressed anxiety.

Post Spiritual Death

You're out there on your own,
Your face turned to stone,
Whatever happened to your life?
Stone Dead Forever[91]

To return to the promised chink of light in the darkness, the black-blue stain on the horizon that may be dawn, what can we do in the face of death? We can, at the very best, take the Nietzschean and Heideggerean approach and to live life as a being that will truly die. To face death in the mirror of one's own face and stand firm; not hopeful, but invigorated. In a short life, we can do little – but we can do more than nothing. That gap between nothing and little is where we have the space to carve out a meaning for our life. Nowhere else. Not in the realm of the spirit, not in the heavens, or post-death worlds, but here and now – with other people, who share this brief window of sentience with us.

An Afterword on Death within Life.

What might it be to take death into oneself? To live openly with the fear, and yet to live – and not be crippled by that death:

Thinking about fear. I had been reading Jim Perrin's 1977 essay *Street Illegal*[92], and was running around a field with it still rattling around my head. In the essay, a young Jim solos[93] some rock in Cheddar, Somerset – unprotected and alone – fuelled by drugs and ennui. At one stage he connects to the wall via a sling and rests – and is overcome by weeping. The fear just seems to have him. So much so that when he completes/survives the climb, he has no joy – barely any feeling is left in him at all. I am reflecting on this fear, and my own mortality and my awareness thereof, when I encounter some regular dog walkers. I don't know them, but I have seen them before with their sleek greyhound-type dogs. I have often noted the unflattering contrast between the effortless gait of the beasts and my own middle-aged lumberings. As I groan past them today, I notice the most sleek of the dogs has bandages and what looks like Clingfilm all around one foot. I catch the eye of the male dog walker (his attractive female companions seem less willing to catch the eye of a sweating stranger in a vest) and he nods at me. He says something, which I half-catch through the music in my ears; the gist is clear – the ailment is a result of ageing. Great. Even that sleekness which mocked my struggling body is itself outrun by time and encroaching mortality. What a fucking great start to the day. I shuffle on.

A minute later, now in a park, running beneath a goalpost that only seems to remind me of when I was so young that I couldn't touch the top of a regulation-sized football goal – even with a jump – the music in my ears changes. Dizzee Rascal's *Fix Up, Look Sharp* blasts at me. It is so full of life. So silly, and youthful, and full of a disregard for seriousness that I cannot help but smile. It makes me feel a fool for my morbid self-absorption.

Here I am, briefly blessed with being alive, not ill, with my body (mostly) working – and out in the world living and breathing and moving. It could have been other music that would have enacted the same mental reversal – some Balkan folk music, or anything life-affirming and raucous – but somehow it reminds me of the squire in Ingrid Bergman's classic film *The Seventh Seal*. Jöns sees the full horror of the world and its inhabitants, but also resists the fall into excessive, speculative agony. Jöns thinks of food, of sex and drink and being alive. He has seen awful things, and the actor (Gunnar Björnstrand) conveys this with real power, but he looks only ahead at the world that he directly encounters- and deals with that in a decisive manner. The world hurts enough without the agony of introspection and the mysteries of faith. I think of Jöns and look directly ahead, and run home – one step nearer to death with every pace – but taking it one step at a time, and glad that I am such a slow runner...

Living Without Spirit

Part 1 – My World
Accounting for the phenomenology
of Being

Those asserting that a non-spiritual account of experience is insufficient to accurately capture the phenomena often describe non-spiritual explanations as 'reductionist'. They point to a variety of human phenomena which they believe to contradict, or at least problematise, such 'reductionist' accounts. Such phenomena include our aesthetic, ascetic, ethical and romantic Inclinations. This does seem to provide a genuine challenge. How can we refuse the use of 'spirit' as an explanatory device, while still holding the evolutionary psychologists at arms-length? Are advocates of the Spirit right to assert that those who would live without it would find themselves intellectually adrift beneath a surplus of meaning and purpose?

Such arguments have been a staple of religious defences against atheism for some time. They are most common in teleological, or design, arguments where it is suggested that if we contrast the Theistic account of how things came to be as they are, with a competing 'reductionist' account, we will discover that the former is able to explain the phenomena of life as we experience it in a more fulsome, holistic and persuasive manner. The widely known 1929[94] book by F. R Tennant entitled *Philosophical Theology* advances just such a view: without Theism explanations for our higher, or deeper, feelings are problematic. [95] How can we account for the feelings evoked in me by great art? What it is that stirs within in me when I am transfixed by the object of my romantic attentions? Why do I feel so much – so much that it seems more than I would 'need' in order to breed and replicate and pass on my (selfish) genes? Surely without either Theism or some world of 'spirit' our explanations become so overwrought and complex that we violate Ockham's razor and must cede the non-material explanatory crown? Such arguments are to be opposed with vigour, as they are as pervasive as they are fallacious. 'Traditional' atheism has long been able to dismiss them for the poor, and somewhat desperate, attempts at reasoning that they represent. Nonetheless, it is worth briefly outlining their primary flaws. To achieve this, I will use as an example the idea of the appreciation of nature that humans have – the common aesthetic, at least, response to it.

Nature and the Spirit: Overpowering the hijackers.

The natural world is an arena where discourses of spirituality reign supreme. The mighty vista, the sense of awe and wonder, the feeling of one's own insignificance in the wider scheme – we are stirred to deeper thoughts. Can we retain depth, and the profound impact on us of being in and with nature, while shedding the need to devalue that very natural world by sublimating it to an external or underlying essence?

The primary problem with claiming that a non-theistic or non-spiritual account fails to fully capture the breadth and depth of human lived experience is that it is both an example of a straw man (or Aunt Sally if you prefer) argument and a fine example of bifurcation. It is a straw man, in that it asserts that those without a religious or spiritual belief wish to 'reduce' their lived experience to an explanation of 'mere' physical mechanics. Two primary issues arise here: the experience at one level (of consciousness, say, of love, or of beauty) does not have to have another level of scale privileged over it and somehow seem as the more 'real' account of what is happening. Even *if* there is a cellular or chemical explanation for the phenomena I experience

– I still have the experience. Knowing that it is generated in a certain manner seems exceptionally, perhaps surprisingly, unable to impact on the quality, the flavour, of my experience. Secondly, the idea that the incredibly complex, nuanced and entrancing nature of conscious states, such as the feelings I have looking across the Cotswolds on a frosty morning, say, are a result of the interaction of forces that we, albeit imperfectly, understand; that they come about from atoms, molecules, proteins, organs and electricity, strikes me not as an account which reduces, but one which imbues the whole process with the character of jaw-dropping awe. This way of understanding our experience does not 'reduce' it to 'mere' naturalistic processes, rather it surely should make us marvel at the good fortune we have to be able to marvel, smell, taste, long and appreciate. As a straw man argument it also is bifucatory in that it suggests that either we concede a world with spirit or God in it (which explains our apparent surplus of meaning), *or* we see the world in this mere mechanistic way. I have outlined one alternative way to view, there may be more, and this by itself refutes such bifucatory posturing.

Everything Happens for a Reason?

People often state this as if causality were a personal discovery of their own – which they feel a need to share with the rest of the world. Of course this is not true. The claim 'everything happens for a reason' is a particular type of causal assertion, which is a reasonable, commonplace one. Were things to happen *without* reasons – the world would be, to borrow the terms of my children's generation 'too random'. Things would just occur, without causes; would pop in and out of existence, and the world would be inexplicable to us, and science would be unable to make any sense of it all. Of course, when we actually, colloquially, hear the phrase 'everything happens for a reason', it is not everyday causality, whether we consider that banal or awe-inspiring, that is being referred to. It is the attribution of additional, unneeded, causal layers to explain or soothe the contingency, mutability and finitude of human existence.

In such violations of Ockham's razor, people cast a web of purpose over the world, such that 'meaning' is inserted at some ontological, pre-perceived level of the world. I would suggest that this is because we are familiar, from religious origins, with the idea that, as the existentialists would put it, *essence precedes existence*. That the world has an intrinsic meaning, that it is *for something* and therefore things in it are part of 'a bigger plan', is a religious mind-set, and one that is difficult for us to shake off. Further to this, shaking it off is painful, for when we see that the explanation of *how* things happen is the same thing as *why* they happen[96], we are finally able to see exactly that which such teleological delusions had obscured from us: our mortality in a world that will forget we ever were. Coping with this does not necessitate putting our head back into the spiritual sand, but there is no question that standing straight in the full knowledge and face of finitude and mortality will require every ounce of fortitude we can muster, and that a non-spiritual, non-materialistic (but materialist), philosophical tradition will have its work cut out helping us stumble on in good faith.

The Contemporary Existentialist's Joyous Burden

The position I have outlined may not be quite so bleakly lonely as we might suspect. In some ways we are knee-deep in post-spiritual ethical resources. Philosophical traditions such as existentialism have sought to find ways of facing up the mere fact of being, without any pre-determining human nature. We can reconsider the existentialist legacy, its interest in humans and their total freedom dispelling the bad-faith, excuse generating fug of contemporary spirituality. In rejecting spiritually derived morality and authority, by working it out, the hard way, in a spiritless world we face the monumental challenge of working things out alone. But we are alone together; just people, with no spirits, angels, collective mind-force, gods or dead ancestors – making the most of a brief window of existence.

If we take what I have said here seriously, then the burden of living a life without notions of spirituality is not to be seen as a mere meaningless drudge through a pointless world. I would go as far as to say that a Nietzschean task of true joy awaits us beyond the heavy velvet curtain of the spirit. This is a task for what I would call 'creative loss', whereby the withdrawal of the spiritual leaves an absence for us to fill ourselves with a world of value and meaning of our choosing. This is a time for true – *thinking* – flow, for dusting ourselves down after our rejection of spirituality and deciding what actually matters, and disputing it amongst us without the danger of spiritual or religious trump cards being played. If Camus can imagine Sisyphus happy, we too can turn our shoulders to the boulder and get stuck into living.

Part 2 – My Response
The Personal and Political in a senseless world

If we truly step beyond a world of spirituality, have the real courage of our convictions, we step into a landscape which might seem featureless, bleak and devoid of the potential for happiness. But this nihilistic dawn is not what it seems. It is what we choose it to be. We are so locked into essentialist accounts of human spirit, of it as a source of value and morals – that even the atheist lives a little in fear of the consequences of their beliefs. These consequences are best provisionally characterised as personal and political. For me – I am burdened by a Sartrean, dreadful, freedom – an accursed liberation – once I move beyond a fixed, or spirit-laden account of my being. I can be anything – but what? Where to start?

I would argue that we start where there is an intersection between the thought of Levinas and those in the mental health professions. That may need some clarification. To begin with the latter; the health of our inner lives[97] seems impacted to a drastic event by a blend of the quantity and quality of our interactions with other living beings, particularly humans. [98] People are good for people – but how might this offer a less bleak perspective on our post-spiritual landscape? If we look at the staggeringly powerful account of Ethics in Levinas we see that the most valuable, centrally human experience comes not from outside us, from a transcendent Lord, nor does it emerge from deep within - as encounter with our 'true' Self. It happens as an experience *between* you and I. The phenomenological, experiential *thing* that happens between me and the Other *is* ethics. It is the potential for an interconnected, rich and humane life. Perhaps how we come to make something of our lives in this bleak, existential wasteland of a post-spiritual world is about how we choose to treat each other. This may seem like very little to go on, in a world bereft of teleological drive, intrinsic meaning and immortal essences, but it is all we have got. It may even turn out to be all we'll ever need.

To reconsider how spirituality lessens or deadens our political instincts is to see this introspective, privatised form of faith writ large. To see how it cocoons us in spiritual preoccupations, and leads us into tunnel vision. There is a substantial concern in alternative spirituality with the environment, but all too often that concern is expressed bereft if it context in broader concerns. Here there is a failure of 'holistic' thinking, and the spiritually interesting categories of environment and gender seem politically privileged – way above such grubby concerns as economic equity and class. It is once more a process a bifurcation, whereby one either adopts a 'spiritual' worldview, or is cast forever as being a mere materialist – concerned only with consumption, money and material gain.

Return to the Pre-Post-Ideological

Metal Interlude: Despite the prevalence in this book of my

seeming opposition to much of what passes in the UK, and beyond, as 'alternative' culture, I am not against a critique of consumerist capitalism. Indeed, my opposition to new-ageism particularly, and contemporary spirituality more broadly, is rooted in its collusion with a culture of consumption. It is not a few on the margins of society to whom this critique applies; for contemporary Mind Body Spirit culture is mainstream. That is what makes its negative fallout so troubling. I am often struck by the pose of evil amongst some outsider groups, and how un-evil they seem by comparison with mainstream culture. I was listening to the song (by Finnish Black Metal band 'Impaled Nazarene') *We're Satan's Generation*, in which they style themselves as 'not giving a fuck', and thinking that actually, despite the band's insistence, they are nowhere near as malign[99] as a shopping centre full of consumers. These consumers, buying sweatshop produced goods, driving four wheel drive SUVs, picking a little Buddha statue maybe, apolitical and not committed to *anything* at all – they truly 'don't give a fuck': Satan wearing chinos and a casual jacket, his arms heavy with goods, his conscience cleared by a post-ideological levity of thought, supplemented by feel-good spirituality. Of course, below the chinos, the aftershave and the tasteful display is anxiety: a sore that no new-age balm can really salve – for it is the total, nihilistic meaningless of their life.

This image of the consumer, driven by anxiety, Neil Young's *Restless Consumer*, pushes us to consider what kind of life would be tolerable? A life that would have more to it than coping strategies, and a retreat into the rabbit hole of personal spirituality? Here there is the need for us to become like a modified Janus. We need to look not in two directions, but switch between two focal lengths: the immediate world of our daily lives and mundane interactions, and that of our mortal nature. We look forwards to our own death, and face it, take what it means seriously and live *as if we are going to die*. The switch to a larger depth of field shows who we share this journey to the grave with: and that we need to spend our time in interaction with each other, not seeking to reach beyond humanity, but living amidst it.

A Thankless Task?

We might begin to get a sense of the post-spiritual on a micro-level, but what about the political? A new post-spiritual politics must be a bleak landscape of fear for the theist, the deist and the spiritual adventurer. It must be a politics that has no truck whatsoever with the Spirit. It is a merciless return to the realm of ideas, of debate, and of truth.

Why must the theist fear our new politics? Because a post-spiritual politics would not merely, in some neo-liberal, faux-neutral gesture, set aside questions of religious truth, but would actively contest the content of theism as it seeks any penetration into the public realm. Over time, a post-spiritual culture cannot countenance any state financial maintenance for religious schools, or recognise religious groups as charitable. This does not rule out sensitive, well-informed Religious Education – the UK has some of the best RE teachers and curricula in the world. Rather it would mean the active promotion of philosophy, of genuine, judgmental, critical faculties which allow people to discriminate with regard to truth claims.

Rituals of the Post-Spiritual

In studying religion over the last two and a half decades, I have widely noted the importance of ritual for practitioners. Many readers will recognise the phenomena of those who have long jettisoned any literal belief in the assertions of a religious tradition, but who persist in their ritual participation. Were I more scurrilous, I might even suggest that this is what underpins the entire non-realist Christian movement[100], but we can certainly see this as preceding the twentieth century, and its challenges to literal faith. The most striking and affective account of this phenomenon can be seen in Balzac's *The Atheist's Mass* where vocal atheist, Desplein, is revealed to be quietly, secretly, attending Mass on a regular basis. This evokes not only a human need, or desire, for ritual, but of course the ability to appreciate art without sharing the world-view which it springs from. [101] With respect to ritual, the open question I here leave hanging is this: does a post-spiritual world need its own rituals?

What might a post-spiritual life-cycle ritual look like? Of course, we have already begun to answer this. Humanist celebrants conduct funerals every day. Some believe in celebrating a girl's first menstruation as an 'entry into womanhood', and for some 'naming ceremonies' replace christenings. These are often based on 'ancient wisdom', but in a secular context are relatively new, but remain, all too often, infected by the spectre of spirituality. However, there is no reason to believe that they will not evolve further. It is clear that if we want rituals, if we need them, then we are as capable of inventing them without spirituality and religion as we have been when we invented them as part of religious traditions.

Post-Spiritual Futures

A post-spiritual way of thinking is not the same as humanism. Humanism often has noble intentions, but regularly appears as a parody of religious groups. The organised British Humanist Association (BHA) could almost be another church, or spiritual group, just one with an absence of theistic content. I do find much of what the BHA says to be persuasive and common-sense, but there is an aspect to Humanism which feels like the historical, liberal political tradition, and its assertions on life as meaningful, and that we survive death in the minds of others, rather trite and pat. Furthermore, the Humanist tradition has defined itself in contrast to, but with close reference to, the forms of institutional theism that dominated at the end of the 19th Century when the BHA was formed, and which persists in disproportionate public influence today. This leaves it, in my view, rather ill equipped to stand as an alternative to the Mind Body Spirit, 'Spiritual but not Religious' views that I have looked at. What is required, though, is something we do indeed find in some contemporary Humanist literature, which is a blend of freedom from dogma *and* a commitment to certain beliefs being true.

What we need in being atheists today is to see it as freedom not only from God, but from the meaningless plurality of new-age inclusivity. The battle with institutional religion has become so bloody, confused and, frankly, pointless, that it has obscured a more immediate threat and opportunity in Western cultures. I have here outlined the threats from generic 'spirituality' to our thinking, our politics and ethics, and to our fulfilment as human beings. However, freedom from Spirituality liberates us in that we escape from being the Zombie-like living-dead of Nietzsche's Last Men; [102] we realise we can respond to the world other than merely with an ironic, world-weary shrug. We are not beyond the ability to actually commit and act if we hold firm to the idea that truth actually matters, is exclusive, and that other people are equally as important as me. This may not bring us the immediate or obvious happiness measurable by 'national well-being' statisticians, but via an existential engagement with life we can at least edge towards knowing what a worthwhile life might look like.

Notes

1) Carrette J, & King, R, *Selling Spirituality*. p.30, Routledge, London, 2005. For anyone interested, they go on to give the kind of well-considered, scholarly and detailed history of the term that I am going to eschew here.

2) Notable in this literature is the British Jesuit journal *The Way*, which describes itself as an 'international journal of contemporary Christian spirituality' which has been regularly published since 1961.

3) To paraphrase the Nicene Creed.

4) Those from the discipline of religious studies will be very familiar with these food-based metaphors for new-age belief construction. I have no intention of resolving here arguments about who did or didn't coin these phrases; though I do feel a slight temptation to proffer a somewhat more liquid metaphor: of new age gurus as cocktail waiters. Into the shaker goes some Buddhism (of course – it like the equivalent of vodka – the base for almost all mixes), a little yoga, some kabala, and – maybe for this recipe – some Eastern Orthodox mysticism, add some ice/contemporary business/MBA psycho-babble and shake. Pour out your creation – name it (Self-actualising a Big Society via Little Changes, maybe?) – and see if the market wants to drink.

5) http://www.cancer.gov/dictionary/?CdrID=441265, Accessed 10/8/2010

6) http://www.naidex.co.uk/NaidexBir11/website/default. aspx?refer=165 Accessed 10/8/2010

7) Ibid

8) Mueller, P S, et al , 'Religious Involvement, Spirituality, and Medicine: Implications for Clinical Practice', *Mayo Clinic Proceedings* December 2001 vol. 76 no. 12 1225-1235 http://www.mayoclinicproceedings.com/content/76/12/1225

.full.pdf

9) Ibid, p.1229

10) Ibid, p.1232. The reference to 'inquiry' is to do with a method of taking a patient's "spiritual history" as part of the identification of spiritual needs.

11) Though I do not believe that there are any good grounds for believing in such things. I take a slightly Sartrean approach of taking my non-belief as a starting point, not a destination in itself. What happens when we take his view that *Existence precedes Essence*? This volume is partly an attempted rehabilitation of existence preceding essence.

12) I will later argue that happiness is a much messier and troubling notion than it usually appears to be.

13) The idea of a 'hobby', while not exclusively so in practice – far from it, seems in its conception peculiarly British. Further, it is often an element in an account of masculinity that is currently passing from the world. I am not sure that kidult 30-somethings playing on their games consoles can be seen as engaging in a 'hobby' in the same way that a man of that age from a previous generation might be in his shed, fashioning model airplanes. As a way of obscuring our sight of our own impending death is not the only way one can, and indeed should, conceive of the social and personal purpose of hobbies. An instructive account of them can be found in Cohen, Stanley & Taylor, Laurie, *Escape Attempts: The Theory and Practice of Resistance to Everyday Life*. Penguin, London, 1976.

14) Not *that* sort of magazines, I mean ones that fit my stereotypical middle-aged man profile: Runners World, Climb, Computer magazines and an array of the very best reading to obscure one's own mortality – catalogues.

15) Carrette and King's *Selling Spirituality* is an entertaining and instructive volume on capitalism and spirituality, and the sidelining of religion.

16) Usually involving the repression of a syncretic pan-religious mysticism.

17) Most notable in Hadot, P., *Philosophy as a Way of Life*. Blackwell, Oxford, 1995.

18) Ibid, p.81ff

19) Ibid, p.103

20) English Standard Version (ESV) Accessed 1/8/11 http://www.biblegateway.com/passage/?search=Ecclesiastes+1&version=ESV

21) Camus, Albert, *The Myth of Sisyphus*. p.11 Penguin, London, 1975.

22) In contrast to some stereotypical renderings, re-reading Camus' *Myth of Sisyphus*, the most notable feature is how positive it is, just how much Camus saw us as able to achieve, if we only knew how.

23) Harpal Jandu Singh – now working on a Masters in Continental Philosophy.

24) Camus, op. cit., p.109

25) Carrette J, & King, R, *Selling Spirituality*. p.32f

26) Ibid, p.40.

27) Heelas, Paul & Woodhead, Linda, *The Spiritual Revolution: Why Religion is Giving Way to Spirituality*. p.27, Blackwell Publishing, Oxford, 2005.

28) And as noted earlier, only some seem able to make sense of the idea, such as Pierre Hadot, leaving me convinced that the term has become almost entirely implicative of a metaphysical or ontological commitment.

29) http://www.snu.org.uk/spiritualism.htm Accessed 1/8/11

30) In the UK, it first blossomed in Yorkshire, having a country wide network of churches by the 1880s. Of course, the Church claims a series of more ancient antecedents. It shares much with the mystics we shall see shortly. It also asserts strong Biblical connections: 'The Christian Church was founded on spirit communication and phenomena that

could be described as mediumship'. http://www.snu.org.
uk/Spiritualism/ancient.htm Accessed 1/8/11

31) A key feature of the new Google Plus service, their attempt
to rival Facebook, is the ability to classify contacts into
'circles', such as friends, colleagues, family and the like:
where the contact is unable to see which circles you hold
them in. Your private mental world of relationships is replicated in digital form, and it *feels* empowering and might be,
where not all your contacts doing the same thing to you. The
point though, is that the designers see customer-value-
recognition in user-implemented customisation.

32) I have chosen a mode of expression for the examples drawn
from Christianity. I could have equally drawn on other
traditions.

33) Published by Bantem Press in 2006

34) This phrase, despite a common misconception to the
contrary, is one that doesn't appear in Kierkegaard's
writings at all, thought the notion fits well enough with
what he *does* write.

35) See Rudolf Otto for theologically respectable version of this
view, in: Otto, Rudolf, *The Idea of the Holy*. Oxford University
Press, Oxford, 1958. He argues that when we encounter the
numinous source of all faith, we do so via a *mysterium
tremendum* that is powerful, and that attempts to articulate
this are the basis of religious faith.

36) Huxley saw it as present in all faiths, but to varying extents.
He describes the *perennial philosophy* as: the metaphysic that
recognizes a divine Reality substantial to the world of things
and lives and minds; the psychology that finds in the soul
something similar to, or even identical with, divine Reality;
the ethic that places man's final end in the knowledge of
the immanent and transcendent Ground of all being; the
thing is immemorial and universal. Rudiments of the
perennial philosophy may be found among the traditional

lore of primitive peoples in every region of the world, and in its fully developed forms it has a place in every one of the higher religions. [Huxley, Aldous *The Perennial Philosophy*, p.vii. Questia eBook: http://www.questia.com/PM.qst?a= o&d=98239109]

37) Ignoring the eradication of many other, non-mystic traditions. Often there is a claim that various forms of paganism and witchcraft, and animistic folk traditions embodied the ancient wisdom of the mystic.

38) Because the approach of literal truth is a male logic of domination and 'penetration of the matter', as opposed to a feminine 'letting be'; Goddess traditions are often keen to self-identify as mystical. This is, of course, lazy and muddled thinking. It represents a type of essentialist gender-analysis which should offend the mind of any feminist who recognises the social, rather than metaphysical, nature of gender construction.

39) Conspiracy theories share many features with some new-age spiritualties, most notable of which is the desire to be a member of the select, wise few – to gain knowledge which other do not have. The general impulse run this: When we discover what is *really* underpinning the *apparent* way in which the world operates, we cease to be members of the 'herd', and transcend to a situation of self-mastery, rather than delusional compliance.

40) Such as in Žižek, Slavoj, *Welcome to the Desert of the Real*. p.12, Verso, London, 2002 – where he talks of the 'thrill of the Real'.

41) This is discussed in Steven Jones' essay *Horrorpron/ Pornhorror*, in Attwood, Feona (ed), *Porn.com*. p131, where he makes the striking claim that: 'perhaps we're so hungry for something genuine that we're willing to suspend disbelief, ingesting even sham authenticity to sate our voyeuristic appetites.'

42) For an almost perfect version of this approach, see http://www.shahriari.com/articles/pub/pub03.htm 1/8/11, which includes the following text: Science has shown that the world is not a giant clock, that God was not a detached clock-maker who made the system and is now watching it operate, and that reducing the system into its constituent parts kills its inherent essence of synergy, and continually makes the truth slip further away from our grasp.

But isn't that what the mystics and philosophers of the past and present have been trying to tell us? Is not the universe one giant cosmic soup of energy which, depending on how we wish to observe it, will manifest into that particular reality?

43) A prime example of this is Bruce Lipton, whose work is full of scientific words. If you look at http://www.brucelipton .com/interviews-with-bruce/ you find the invocation of fractal geometry, cell membranes, and more. I do not wish to dispute his science, or results, here, but at the same URL wish to merely note the sentence below as paradigmatic of science/spirit discourse's self-characterisation:

My research revealed a revolutionary understanding of how life 'worked' twenty years ago and this awareness is now beginning to be recognized by leading edge science.

44) *Bhagavad Gita* IX, 23-24 in Zaehner, *Hindu Scriptures.* p.288, J. M. Dent, London, 1966.

This view is also represented elsewhere in the Bhagavad-Gita, see: *Bhagavad Gita* IV, 11.

45) Udana 6.4, *The Tittha Sutta*, where the image of blind-men, who have only felt part of the elephant, argue as to whether it is more like a snake, or a tree trunk. What is notable, of course, is that the Buddha wishes to assert that it is only *other* sages who this partial view –and that he sees the whole elephant! As Bhikkhu Thanissaro translates the phrase near the end of the Sutta: In the same way, monks, the wanderers

of other sects are blind and eyeless. They don't know what is beneficial and what is harmful. They don't know what is the Dhamma and what is non-Dhamma. Not knowing what is beneficial and what is harmful, not knowing what is Dhamma and what is non-Dhamma, they live arguing, quarreling, and disputing, wounding one another with weapons of the mouth, saying, 'The Dhamma is like this, it's not like that. The Dhamma's not like that, it's like this.' [http://www.accesstoinsight.org/tipitaka/kn/ud/ud.6.04.tha n.html]

46) The third version Aristotle gives of 'his' second law of thought, in his *Metaphysics*.

47) Within self-described pagan communities, this term has a more specific meaning, which it does not harm to entirely ignore here.

48) See Derrida on 'Phallogocentrism' As the (ever-wonderful) peer-reviewed Internet Encyclopaedia of Philosophy notes: Logocentrism emphasises the privileged role that *logos*, or speech, has been accorded in the Western tradition. Phallogocentrism points towards the patriarchal signifi- cance of this privileging. [Jack Reynolds, La Trobe University http://www.iep.utm.edu/derrida/]

49) Penny, Laurie, *Meat Market: Female Flesh Under Capitalism*. p.45, Zero Books, Winchester UK, 2010.

50) The Gaia hypothesis is easily assimilated into the Nature- Goddess discourse of neo-paganism.

51) Note that I am refraining from the rhetorical strategy I earlier condemned, of invoking these texts on the basis of their 'ancient wisdom'. I mention them as they seem to be not only the earliest (maybe 3rd Century BCE), but also until recent psychology, the most thorough attempt to systemati- cally engage with the contents of human consciousness. I am ransacking them for their intellectual content, not as a badge of authenticity!

52) Much of what I say here may seem much more Rinzai, than Sōtō, as pertains to Zen, but the distinction is rarely as simple as it seems. The zazen, just-sitting, approach of Sōtō Zen may seem even less thoughtful, but can actually be seen as a form of very powerful thought training – it is not about any kind of spirituality, but about training oneself in thought. Many would dispute this vociferously, and this is not the place to get overly drawn, but I would probably begin via a pro-thought reading of Dōgen's *Bendowa*.

53) Those wishing to engage with *koans* could do much better than the famous 'one hand clapping', and turn to *The Blue Cliff Record*.

54) Bashō is the most famous writer of Zen *haiku* for a reason, and always delivers. I would also recommend the poetry of Ryōkan, not merely for aesthetic reasons, but because of its seeming total un-reliance on the invocation of the spiritual.

55) Carrette and King remark on the combination of the 'privatisation' of faith (also noted by sociologists of religion with respect to mainstream faiths in many Western cultures) and 'New Age Individualism'. *Ibid*, p.95f.

56) Stark, Rodney & Sims Bainbridge, William, *The Future of Religion: Secularization, Revival and Cult Formation.* p.210, University of California Press, London, 1985.

57) http://www.statistics.gov.uk/downloads/theme_compendia /for2004/FocusonReligion.pdf

58) 'Man is by nature a political animal'. (I.1253a2 – This is a Bekker Number reference)

59) In the absence of a better word. I recoil somewhat from this usage, but bow in the face of its pervasive colloquial deployment.

60) Most mythic is perhaps the avowed refusal of judgement, or stance thereof. How often might we hear someone say that a friend is someone who 'doesn't judge me', and maintain that 'I don't judge' is one of your best personality traits; while

also being entirely located within both personal and cultural nexuses of judgement? Is it even possible not to judge friends? In a culture where every gesture, clothing and other display is so deeply codified by fashion, wealth, taste and class – we judge with an astonishing level of nuance. It hardly needs stating that contemporary TV is largely a story of the growth of judgement. We even get to vote about it, as judges by proxy, in reality TV; or conspire with arch voiceovers to judge how little self-insight the TV version of friends have, in shows like *Come Dine with Me.*

61) http://www.gazette.de/Archiv/Gazette-August2001/Zizek 2.html

62) There is a disreputable bifurcation at work here, implying that either you seek change in the world OR in yourself. It also implies a very hard-edged border between my self and the world; odd when parallel discourses often seek to namecheck notions of interdependence.

63) Cynical in that we don't believe in such fictions anymore – the postmodernist is rather miserable than naive, and our fetishished wisdom, a bastardised misreading of Buddhism and Stoicism, makes us wary of actually enjoying things – too alive to the dangers and temporality of pleasure.

64) Despite what you may suspect, and despite its widespread abuse, the term 'holistic' is actually a very valuable one – once wrested free from its new-age kidnappers.

65) http://www.guardian.co.uk/politics/2010/nov/14/david-cam eron-wellbeing-inquiry accessed 27/7/11

66) Ehrenreich, Barbara, *Smile or Die.* Granta, London, 2009, p.12-13

67) Layard, Richard, *Happiness: Lessons From a New Science.* Penguin, London, 2005.

68) http://www.actionforhappiness.org/why-happiness cites Bentham, Mill and Singer. That might give us a clue as to their philosophical stance.

69) http://www.actionforhappiness.org/10-keys-to-happier-living

70) http://www.actionforhappiness.org/ Accessed 16/8/11

71) In the case of Action for Happiness, its founders seem to draw, in new-age syncretic style, on Utilitarianism and their readings of Yoga, Buddhism and the Positive Psychology movement.

72) For some interesting work on what it means to be happy, which actually acknowledges the detail of Greek ideas, and their engagement with questions of finitude, see the blog of Jules Evans at http://www.politicsofwellbeing.com/

73) Seneca, *Epistula Morales* I.17, Cited in [i] Dollimore, J., *Death, Desire & Loss in Western Culture*, p.25. Penguin, Lodon, 1998.

74) http://emotionsblog.history.qmul.ac.uk/?p=83 for an overview. The report can be seen at https://www.education.gov.uk/publications/standard/publicationDetail/Page1/DFE-RR097

75) This quote is, for reasons I cannot discover, often misattributed online, to Heidegger himself. Lavine, T. Z., *From Socrates to Sartre: The Philosophic Quest*. Bantam, 1984.

76) One writer, in one of those 'big idea' tomes typical of the period (first published in the USA in 1973, two years before Philippe Ariès' *Essais sur l'histoire de la mort en Occident: du Moyen Âge à nos jours.*) suggests that all human civilisation is an attempt to deal with the human knowledge that we shall each die: and this still is not enough to fully hide it from ourselves. See Becker, Ernest, *The Denial of Death*. Souvenir Press, London, 2011.

77) Bradley, Ben, *Well-Being and Death*. OUP, Oxford 2009, p.xiii

78) Ibid.

79) Plato, *Phaedo,* http://classics.mit.edu/Plato/phaedo.html, accessed 9/8/2010

80) Bradley cites *Phado* 64a

81) Plato, *Phaedo,* http://classics.mit.edu/Plato/phaedo.html,

accessed 9/8/2010

82) Be that as art, culture or politics.

83) As he writes: Thus death reveals itself as that *possibility which is one's ownmost, which is non-relational, and which is not to be outstripped.* BT251 Heidegger, Martin, *Being and Time.* p.294, Blackwell, Oxford, 1962.

84) See http://www.telegraph.co.uk/health/healthnews/716885 6/Ageing-gene-found-by-scientists-could-be-key-to-longer-lifespans.html. While there are good grounds for believing there are genetic factors int eh ageing process, the that hugely increased lifespans are available via the manipulation of a single gene is clearly as naive, superficial and simplistic as newspaper stories about the 'gay gene', and various others, but equally seems like a archetypically media-led approach to science (That is, it can lead with 'Scientists discover' – as though it is through intermittent empirical epiphanies that science lurches forward)

85) Of course, these stories also compete for column inches with ones claiming that the current generation of young people, due to obesity and inactive lifestyles, will be the first for centuries to see a rapid decline in life expectancy. The paper most keen on longevity stories seems rather keen, oddly, on these stories too: such as the headine: 'Generation 'could die before their parents' as avoidable health complaints soar.' [http://www.dailymail.co.uk /health/article-1265600/Generation-die-parents-avoidable-health-complaints-soar.html] but like the longevity stories, are also found in the 'quality' press: ' Children will die before their parents' [http://www.guardian.co.uk/ politics/2004/may/27/health.foodanddrink]

86) http://www.dailymail.co.uk/sciencetech/article-557656/Why-man-COULD-live-Desmond-Morris.html Also see http://www.dailymail.co.uk/health/article-1314524/Fou ntain-youth-pill-just-years-shop-shelves.html and http://

www.dailymail.co.uk/sciencetech/article-1319011/Eternal-youth-Is-science-brink-creating-elixir-life.html

87) http://www.independent.co.uk/news/science/who-wants-to-live-for-ever-a-scientific-breakthrough-could-mean-humans-live-for-hundreds-of-years-772418.html

88) The tabloid press rather like him. For example see http://www.dailymail.co.uk/sciencetech/article-2011425/The-person-reach-150-alive — soon-live-THOUSAND-claims-scientist.html. To be fair to him, he has tended to steer away from longevity claims a little in some more recent interviews, rather concentrating on better health in old age, but even so his recent claim in a Guardian interview that 'I think we're in striking distance of keeping people so healthy that at 90 they'll carry on waking up in the same physical state as they were at the age of 30' [http://www.guardian.co.uk/technology/2010/aug/01/aubrey-de-grey-ageing-research] still seems wholly speculative

89) Gray, John, *The Immortalization Commission*. P. 236. Allen Lane, 2011.

90) Most notably chronicled by Philippe Ariès, in books such as *The Hour of Our Death*. Alfred a Knopf Ltd, 1981.

91) Motörhead, *Stone Dead Forever* (from the Album *Bomber* 1979)

92) Collected in: Perrin, Jim, *The Climbing Essays*. pp29-30, The In Pinn, Glasgow, 2009

93) Climbs without ropes, or any other protection.

94) With a second volume in 1930

95) Tennant claims that the tenants of contemporary science constitute a: fictional descriptive scheme, or rather an incongruous set of schemes, partially applicable, into all or any of which even inorganic Nature refuses wholly to fit. [Tennant, F. R., *Philosophical Theology* Vol 2, p.51, CUP, 1930]

96) This how/why trope is a staple of religious reflection, such as BBC Radio 4's *Thought for the Day*. Here a religious figure

will explain that although science can give us the 'how' things are, it takes a faith tradition to answer the 'why' of life. This is staggeringly presumptive – as it takes for granted that there *are* 'why' questions left unanswered by the 'how'. In so doing, in presuming its conclusion in its premises, it is a clear case of question-begging.

97) For a sensitive and well-grounded use of ideas of 'wellbeing; and of a no-spiritual approach to the possible benefits of mindfulness meditation, it is worth looking at the website of the Mental Health Foundation: http://www.mentalhealth.org.uk/

98) There are rather intriguing animal therapy approaches – and some animals (cats, say, as opposed to a house of chicken) seem very powerful at affecting human stress – although I would be interested in how much nervous, mentally ill humans stress out otherwise-chilled cats...

99) They delighted, I thought, in bans in parts of the EU related to a certain strand of Finnish nationalism, which they rejected not though articulating a different politics, but by claiming to have no interest in it all: as though this the safest policy, or most efficacious rebuttal. I think, and even titles like *Goat Vomit and Gas Masks* can't convince me otherwise, that they are idiots, but the self-promotion of oneself as 'evil' struck a chord for me.

100) For more on this movement, see the Sea of Faith network.

101) This second point seems obvious, but is surprisingly often something challenged. My atheism does not preclude my enjoyment of a requiem mass, or of religious paintings, or my appreciation of religious architecture. I can be an atheist and still be moved by a hymn, just as I can enjoy Black Metal without actually pledging my life to Satan. This seems, as I say, staggeringly obvious, but some seem to feel that in rejecting a religion as an embodiment of empirical truth, one is required to reject all aesthetic and cultural

phenomena that have been affiliated with it.

102) In Hollingdale's translation, we find them rendered as 'the Ultimate men: '"We have discovered happiness," say the last men, and blink...No herdsman, and one herd' Nietzsche, Friedrich, *Thus Spoke Zarathustra.* p.46, Penguin, London, 1961

Contemporary culture has eliminated both the concept of the public and the figure of the intellectual. Former public spaces – both physical and cultural – are now either derelict or colonized by advertising. A cretinous anti-intellectualism presides, cheerled by expensively educated hacks in the pay of multinational corporations who reassure their bored readers that there is no need to rouse themselves from their interpassive stupor. The informal censorship internalized and propagated by the cultural workers of late capitalism generates a banal conformity that the propaganda chiefs of Stalinism could only ever have dreamt of imposing. Zer0 Books knows that another kind of discourse – intellectual without being academic, popular without being populist – is not only possible: it is already flourishing, in the regions beyond the striplit malls of so-called mass media and the neurotically bureaucratic halls of the academy. Zer0 is committed to the idea of publishing as a making public of the intellectual. It is convinced that in the unthinking, blandly consensual culture in which we live, critical and engaged theoretical reflection is more important than ever before.